Navigate

How to Know
God's Purposes for Our Lives

Jay Simala

Navigate: How to Know God's Purposes for Our Lives

Copyright © 2020 by "Jay" Joseph P. Simala

All rights reserved. No part of this publication may be reproduced or transmitted in any form or by any means, including electronic, mechanical, photocopying, recording, or any other, except for brief quotations in printed reviews, without prior written permission of the author. However, the author makes some of this material available at JaySimala.com/documents. You are permitted to reproduce and transmit, but not alter, those documents.

ISBN: 978-1-7344800-2-3 (paperback)

ISBN: 978-1-7344800-3-0 (e-book)

Unless otherwise noted, all Scripture quotations have been taken from the Christian Standard Bible®, Copyright © 2017 by Holman Bible Publishers. Used by permission. Christian Standard Bible® and CSB® are federally registered trademarks of Holman Bible Publishers.

Design by Renée Yearwood/reneeyearwood.com

Copyediting by Christi McGuire/christimcguire.com

To my brothers and sisters in Christ at New Song,
who love God and love people.

Contents

* Prioritize reading these lessons if you want to begin with an overview of the book.

About the Author and His Website 8

This Series 9

Introduction 18

Unit One: We Are Christians 33

    Overview 35

    1. Adopted* 36

    2. Declared Righteous* 40

    3. Set Apart 44

    4. Alive 48

    5. Chosen 52

    Guide for Meeting with Others 56

Unit Two: We Are Growing into the Likeness of Jesus 61

    Overview 63

    6. Stand Strong through Your Trials* 64

    7. Run with Endurance* 68

    8. Confirm Your Calling 72

    9. Focus on Jesus Christ 76

    10. Walk by the Holy Spirit 80

    Guide for Meeting with Others 84

Unit Three: We Serve Those in Need 89
  Overview...91
  11. Work at Your God-Given Responsibilities 92
  12. Give Financially* 96
  13. Use Your Spiritual Gifts* 100
  14. Love Your Neighbor 104
  15. Care for Creation..108
  Guide for Meeting with Others 112

Unit Four: We Help Non-Christians to Know God.................117
  Overview...119
  16. Take the Gospel Message to Others 120
  17. Introduce People to God the Father* 124
  18. Explain and Confront Sin* 128
  19. Proclaim and Explain the Gospel* 132
  20. Proclaim Repentance and Forgiveness* 136
  Guide for Meeting with Others 140

Unit Five: We Help Christians to Know God Better.................145
  Overview...147
  21. Make Disciples* 148
  22. Explain the Meaning of Following Jesus* 152
  23. Direct Others to God's Word 156
  24. Teach Others to Pray...160
  25. Teach the Truth..164
  Guide for Meeting with Others 168

Unit Six: We Center Our Lives on God (Part One) 173
    Overview 175
    26. Listen to God 176
    27. Pray to God 180
    28. Trust in God* 184
    29. Hope in God 188
    30. Love God* 192
    Guide for Meeting with Others 196

Unit Seven: We Center Our Lives on God (Part Two) 201
    Overview 203
    31. Imitate God 204
    32. Worship God* 208
    33. Glorify God* 212
    34. Enjoy God 216
    35. Obey God 220
    Guide for Meeting with Others 224

References 228
Acknowledgments 230

About the Author and His Website

Jay is husband to Lyndsey and father of four children. He is also a pastor and an educator in universities—both in the areas of Christian ministries and organizational leadership.

He completed degrees in pastoral ministry (MDiv) and in counseling-psychology (MA) from Trinity Evangelical Divinity School, in business (BBA and MBA) from the University of Wisconsin, and in higher education (PhD) from Loyola University Chicago.

Visit him at **JaySimala.com**. There you will find:

- Free PDFs of select two-page lessons from this book that you can use with others, whether for one-on-one meetings, in Bible studies, or when teaching larger groups.
- Recommendations for how to develop basic habits for Christian growth, such as Bible reading and prayer.
- Guidance for how to create and follow a study plan of Christian resources.
- Access to his videos and other content.
- How to contact him.

Please feel free to take advantage of these resources and contact him with comments and questions.

This Series

Overview

Christian Guidebooks is the name of a series of books that helps you walk more closely with God and live out his purposes for your life—particularly in your family and in a local church.

Each book has thirty-five two-page lessons to make the topics as clear and accessible as possible, which are **grouped together in seven units**. In addition to the individual lessons, in each book I include **seven unit overviews, "For Reflection and Discussion" questions** (at the end of each two-page lesson), and **seven guides for meeting with others** to help you talk more openly with others who want to learn more about God.

As you read, set aside enough time in your life to pray about and discuss what God is teaching you, ideally with others in a local church.

Together, these books outline a comprehensive approach to thinking and living as a Christian.

Detailed Explanation

As a pastor and an educator, I consistently have the privilege of helping those who want to connect more deeply with God—the God who speaks to us through the Bible.

In those settings and others, I have observed that while many people want to learn more about God, they struggle as they relate to him. The most unsettled ones often have these things in common:

- They believe in Jesus, but it is not always clear what that means to them, nor if that makes any practical difference in their lives.
- They are not certain if they will spend eternity with God. However, they believe they are well on their way to earning eternal life with him, but there is more work to do—some finishing touches in their moral development.

- They are not clear regarding what mission God has for their lives or why they ultimately exist. Related, they lack the confidence (or the desire) to help others mature in the Christian faith.
- They admit they lack a basic knowledge of the Bible, even if they were raised in Christian homes. Digging deeper, I learn that their personal Bible reading is often dull and sporadic.
- They are sincere and well-meaning. They show good intent—in their romantic relationships, as parents, or at work. They want to live with integrity, though they are not sure how to integrate their faith into their lives more fully.

Does this describe you? Or people you know?

I decided to write this series, Christian Guidebooks, to help you address challenges like these, in your own life or in the lives of those you love.

Ultimately, I am writing these books for two reasons.

1. To Help You to Know God

I want to help you to know the God of the Bible, whether you come to know him for the first time or in a more personal way.

God is one being, existing eternally as three persons (Father, Son, and Holy Spirit). He offers us the gift of eternal life, which we receive by turning from our sin and trusting in Jesus.

In a prayer directed to God the Father, Jesus said:

> "This is eternal life: that they may know you, the only true God, and the one you have sent—Jesus Christ." (John 17:3; see also John 14:17)

The Holy Spirit and the Word of God guide people to those ends (John 15:26; Acts 10:44; 1 Cor. 2:13; 1 Thess. 1:5–6; 1 Pet. 1:23).

2. To Help You to Make God Known

I also want to equip you to help others to know God. The apostle Paul clarified both our calling and message:

Therefore, we are ambassadors for Christ, since God [the Father] is making his appeal through us. We plead on Christ's behalf: "Be reconciled to God [the Father]." (2 Cor. 5:20)

Whether in our families, our churches, or anywhere else, God the Father calls us to help others to know him through Jesus Christ. Christians make disciples (or followers) of Jesus—proclaiming, in particular, the good news that he died and rose from the dead (Matt. 28:18–20; Luke 24:44–49; Acts 1:8; 1 Cor. 15:1–4). To know the God of the Bible is to love him. And one of the most profound ways we express that love is by helping others to know him as well.

What do these books have in common?

1. These books are designed to help you grow in your relationship with God.

Do you want to learn or review the basic truths of the Christian faith? Or, if you are already well established, do you want help in passing along your faith to others?

Either way, these books consistently encourage you in the following ways:

- to know, love, and obey the triune God of the Bible: Father, Son, and Holy Spirit.
- to study the Bible, which reveals God's will for our lives.
- to view yourself and your life from God's perspective, including your sinful choices.
- to embrace Jesus's life, death, and resurrection as essential to your relationship with God.
- to live under the lordship of Jesus, which includes living in light of his second coming to the earth.
- to choose godly character and godly actions, even in the midst of pain and suffering.
- to serve wisely within your sphere of influence, particularly in your family and in a local church.

- to equip you to contribute to the mission of the church—to make disciples (or followers) of Jesus Christ.
- to be God-centered in all you do, particularly in faith, hope, love, and worship.
- to submit to the work of the Holy Spirit, who guides and empowers Christians to do God's will.

I encourage you in these ways because they are God's desires for each of us. The Bible makes that clear.

2. These books are arranged as a progression.

As you seek to mature in your faith, and given the vast number of Christian books and websites, it is natural to ask questions like these: What topics should I study? In what order? How do I then take what I have learned and help others to develop in their faith?

With questions like these in mind, I organize the books as a progression, with each book setting a foundation for the next. For example, the first book in the series helps you establish or reestablish your relationship with God. The second book then helps you set the direction of your life by studying God's purposes for his people as outlined in the Bible.

Therefore, I recommend that you study the books in order, particularly if you consider yourself relatively young in the Christian faith or if you are mentoring someone in that category. However, each book does stand alone, so begin where you like.

3. These books are structured to make the Bible accessible.

Each lesson within the books is two pages long, with the goal of presenting biblical truths as clearly and concisely as possible.

Lord willing, this series will contain hundreds of two-page lessons, each designed for you to discuss with others (see #4 below).

Lesson topics (though not necessarily the lesson titles) include:

- Establishing Habits of Bible Reading and Prayer

- Recognizing the Significance of God as Our Creator
- Identifying and Overcoming Sin in Your Life
- Embracing Jesus's Mission for Our Lives
- Learning How to Walk Closely with the Holy Spirit
- Introducing Others to God through Jesus Christ
- Choosing Joy in the Midst of Pain

Each book follows a consistent structure: seven units, with five two-page lessons per unit, for a total of thirty-five lessons per book.

4. These books are designed to help you connect and serve within a local church.

I encourage you to read these books with others, ideally with those in your local church—whether they are your church leaders, your spiritual peers, or individuals you want to mentor. We simply cannot mature in the Christian faith apart from authentic, biblically-informed relationships within a local church.

Why such an emphasis on the local church? God instructs his people to participate actively in the life of a local church and its leaders (Heb. 10:24–25; 13:7, 17). It is there that we partner together to pursue God's purposes (Acts 2:42–47; 4:32–37; Phil. 1:3–5).

When we join a church, we commit to a local body of Christians for the purposes of worship, making followers of Jesus Christ, serving others, mutual encouragement, and much more.

These books, therefore, direct you repeatedly to life and meaning and ministry in a church. If you have not done so already, choose a church that proclaims, explains, and applies the Bible—one that centers itself on Jesus Christ.[1] You will never regret establishing deep roots there.

---

[1] See Mark Dever's book *What Is a Healthy Church?* for guidance.

5. These books are oriented toward learning.

There are no shortcuts for growing in our relationship with God and others. However, one of the most difficult challenges for all of us is learning to slow down to read the Bible, to discuss what God is teaching us, and to pray.

Instead, we often surf or skim our way from one topic to the next, and therefore we see little change in our lives. But we will mature in the faith in direct proportion to the extent that we make time.

Study these books at the pace that works best for you. Here are two suggestions for how to use the material:

a. Study each unit of five lessons with others.

Whether you study with others one-on-one, in a small group, or in a classroom setting, here is a suggestion for how to work through each unit *in a period of seven days*:

- Day 1: Read the unit overview.
- Days 1–5: Study one two-page lesson per day for five days. After each lesson, use the two pages labeled "For Reflection and Discussion" to respond to the questions, record your prayers to God, and/or prepare to process the information with others.
- Days 1–7: Memorize one or more of the suggested memory verses and/or other verses of your choosing.
- Days 6 and 7: Within the "Guide for Meeting with Others," which you will find after each grouping of five lessons, complete the items under "For Discussion." Use the pages labeled "Notes" to prepare for your meeting.
- Day 7: Meet with one or more fellow Christians using the guide to provide structure.

Or study one unit with others *every two weeks*, which allows you to finish one of these books in fourteen weeks—or sixteen weeks if you devote one meeting to discussing the introduction (which I recommend).

b. Study one lesson at a time with others.

I often use the two-page lessons when meeting one-on-one with others, in group Bible studies, or when teaching classes in a church, leaving at least 25% of the time for discussion, application, and prayer. I make many of the lessons available for you to print and share at JaySimala.com/documents.

Regardless of the approach you use, you will learn according to your willingness to process the material thoroughly and to do so with others.

6. These books are based on the Bible.

God speaks to us in and through the Bible (2 Tim. 3:16; 2 Pet. 1:20–21). From the beginning of our relationship with God, his Word gives us the instruction and encouragement we need to begin, to continue, and to finish well. With this in mind, these books focus on the Bible with the hope that your love for and obedience to the God of the Bible will grow.

For your Bible reading and study, I encourage you to use a study Bible, such as:

- *ESV Study Bible (ESVSB)*,
- *NIV Biblical Theology Study Bible (NIVBTSB)*,[2] or
- *CSB Study Bible (CSBSB)*.[3]

As you read Bible passages in my books, pause to read the corresponding notes at the bottom of the page in your study Bible.

For all of us, the goal is to move closer to the meaning of God's words in Scripture and therefore closer to the God who stands

---

[2] This study Bible was previously published with the title *NIV Zondervan Study Bible*. The content did not change with the new title.

[3] Jesus has been kind to provide his church with the gifted teachers in these works (Eph. 4:11–13). I am grateful.

behind those words. Oh, that each of us would receive the Word with eagerness and examine the Scriptures daily (Acts 17:11)!

7. These books are centered on God.

To close out this section where we began, God is simultaneously one God (Deut. 6:4; Isa. 44:6) and three persons: Father, Son, and Holy Spirit (Matt. 28:19; Eph. 2:18; Rev. 1:4–5). This is the Holy Trinity of the Christian faith.

The biblical authors worked diligently to highlight each member of the Trinity. Once you see that, your Bible reading will never be the same.

Therefore, as we read the Bible, we should determine what we can learn about each person of the Trinity (including personal attributes, words, and actions) in a given passage.

For example, in the words of the apostle Paul:

> In him [Jesus] you also were sealed with the promised Holy Spirit when you heard the word of truth, the gospel of your salvation, and when you believed. The Holy Spirit is the down payment of our inheritance, until the redemption of the possession, to the praise of his [God the Father's] glory. (Eph. 1:13–14)

The center of the New Testament, in particular, is God the Father working in and through the person, words, and works of Jesus Christ (Matt. 28:18; John 5:19; 12:49; 2 Cor. 5:19; Eph. 1:3–12; Col. 1:15–20; Heb. 1:1–2; Jude 24–25; Rev. 19:11–21). To each we express our love and worship (Matt. 22:37–38; John 14:15; Rev. 5:13–14).

It is the Holy Spirit who helps us to see and savor these truths and then to live accordingly (John 3:5–7; 15:26; Acts 7:55; Gal. 5:22–23; Phil. 3:3).[4]

---

[4] In his *New Testament Theology*, Thomas Schreiner states that New Testament "theology is God-focused, Christ-centered, and Spirit-saturated" (23).

As I write, I want to make all of this clear so you can see it and help others to see it as well.

A Word about My Choice of Language

I most often refer to the first person of the Trinity as "God" or "God the Father." When I refer to him as "God the Father," it is because that is the most common way Christians distinguish him from the second and third persons of the Trinity.

I most often refer to the second and third persons of the Trinity, respectively, as "Jesus Christ" and "the Holy Spirit," both of whom are fully God in essence (John 1:1; Acts 5:3–4). Again, I do this for ease of identification and for consistency.

Introduction

Before my wife and I had children, we had freedom—to spend a bit more money for recreation, to experience consistent peace and quiet in our home, and to travel more regularly.

So early in our marriage we took a trip in the Boundary Waters Canoe Area Wilderness of Minnesota. As I tell the story below, Lyndsey shares her own perspectives of our vacation in the footnotes of this section.[5]

One of my primary goals was to impress Lyndsey with my leadership and navigation skills. I knew of men, whether real or fictional, who distinguished themselves on or under the high seas. For example:

- Fleet Admiral Chester W. Nimitz was a brilliant and decisive naval leader. The USS Nimitz supercarrier was named for him.[6]
- Captain Marko Ramius masterfully commanded a Soviet submarine through the depths of the North Atlantic Ocean in Tom Clancy's novel *The Hunt for Red October*.[7]
- Skipper from the TV show *Gilligan's Island* demonstrated fearless courage, guiding the S.S. Minnow and her passengers to safety.[8]

How would history remember me? What would be my legacy?

The sun burned hot the first two days. We spent six hours the first day and then ten hours the second day rowing through lakes and rivers. Though the waters were calm and there was little wind,

---

[5] Hi, friends, I'm Lyndsey! For the record, I wanted to take a cruise to Alaska or go to a tropical beach.

[6] Is Jay preparing to compare himself to Admiral Nimitz? My apologies to all who have served in the navy—or, for that matter, any branch of the military.

[7] A Soviet submarine captain in the depths of the North Atlantic Ocean? My goal was to stay above the water with a Polish husband in the shallow lakes of Minnesota. God help me.

[8] Okay, this comparison actually fits: both Skipper (on the show) and Jay (in real life) have slightly rounded bellies. And I do like the theme song of *Gilligan's Island*.

I was exhausted by the second night of the trip. I begged Lyndsey to let me stay at the campsite for thirty-six hours so I could recover.[9]

Also, given that I did not wear a shirt those first two days, and given that I have small belly rolls of fat when I am sitting down, when I stood up, I had sunburn marks that ran horizontally across my stomach. With a red marker, the sun highlighted my abs of jelly.[10]

Even when I was well-rested, carrying a canoe between lakes and rivers, which is called *portaging*, was a challenge for both of us. One of the portages was more than one-fourth mile long, and I wore my rain jacket to protect myself from the Jay-eating mosquitoes.

Lyndsey is about 100 pounds when she is holding a brick or two, so she impressed me by her ability to carry a 50-pound pack by herself. At one point her pack pulled her straight back, and she landed in the brush, a helpless turtle stuck on her back. Realizing that Lyndsey desperately needed me, I felt a rush of strength come over me. I helped her to her feet, but only after waiting a few minutes to consider what a great leader would do.[11]

Setting our course and staying on course were the most significant challenges of the trip. Lyndsey and I took turns reading the map, and we both struggled at points. It took time to understand the scale of the map in relationship to the geographical markers. Fortunately, we only took one or two wrong turns during the trip, and it was relatively easy to get back on course.

The weather turned against us the final two days. Early one evening, while traveling through one of the bigger lakes on our

---

[9] I agreed to give him time to recover. My other option was to secure a fishing line in his mouth and tow him behind the canoe.
[10] I told you that Jay has a rounded belly, didn't I? But given the sunburn marks ran horizontally, from a distance you would have thought he had a six-pack.
[11] Jay actually helped me immediately—a wise choice. However, if I remember correctly, he first wanted to take my picture—not a wise choice.

route, we got caught in a rainstorm. I was not skilled enough to keep the canoe straight, which was my job since I was steering. The wind pushed us aground, so I had to drag the canoe along the shoreline until we got to our campsite. I was soaked and started to shiver in the tent. Because all my clothes got wet, I wore one of Lyndsey's shirts to stay warm.[12]

On the final morning, we traveled on the Kawishiwi River through another storm. The wind again pushed us ashore and, worse, in circles. This again reflected my inability to keep the canoe straight.

I quickly got angry with myself. But to protect myself psychologically and to shift blame, I became frustrated with Lyndsey, who was patiently spinning away.[13] *Why was her rowing so wimpy? Why wasn't she providing me with emotional support? Why must I suffer righteously?* I didn't voice my frustrations, but I was ready to abandon ship.[14] Hours later, we reached the exit point.[15]

As I reflect back on that vacation, I realize that I will never have a legacy as a decisive leader of the high seas or the still waters. No boat will ever bear my name, like the USS Nimitz. Alas, just recently, as I considered writing my name on my youngest daughter's rubber duckie, my older daughter yanked it out of my hand. *My rubber duckie.*[16]

Setting and Maintaining Our Course in Life

During the canoe trip, the obstacles I faced were obvious: my own lack of skill, lack of strength, and lack of humility.

In the midst of my struggles, I was grateful for my wife, for she brought joy and perspective into each part of the trip. It reminded

---

[12] Jay is 6 feet, 6 inches, and I am 5 feet, 2 inches. So while the shirt didn't fit, Jay looks reasonably good in delicate colors.
[13] That's called psychological displacement, but he later apologized.
[14] For my part, I stayed fairly calm. I like merry-go-rounds, whether on land or on the water. Whee!
[15] I love you, but never again, Captain Jay.
[16] Good for you, sweet girl. Lyndsey here, signing off. God be with you!

me that God designed all of us to live in community, both to give and to receive help through life's challenges.

I was also grateful for the map. Throughout the trip, it was our focal point. It marked every lake, river, and land mass, and it was drawn to scale. Even when we got lost and when other challenges surfaced, the map was a stable, reliable guide to get us back on course.

As it relates to setting and maintaining our course in life, the Bible provides the map for us. Most importantly, it explains how to know God through Jesus Christ, who described himself as the way to God the Father (John 14:6). From this perspective, once we turn from our sin and trust in Jesus, we have already arrived at the final destination: a reconciled relationship with God himself (Rom. 5:10).

From a different perspective, there is still much walking, or paddling, to do in this life (1 Thess. 2:12; Col. 2:6; Gal. 5:16). In this regard, the Bible provides the map that explains how we can obey God. In the process of studying the Bible, we learn about the purposes God has established for us, such as sharing our faith with others and worshiping him. Even though each path is not marked, the Bible guides us as we navigate our way to the end of the trip.

But I have found that many Christians do not have a clear sense of what God has already done in their lives and what God wants them to do.

To help people think through these issues, I lead church groups and university students through the following activity—an activity I encourage you to do with people in your own life.

I say:

> Whether you write on a piece of paper
> or type your answer on a computer,
> complete this sentence:
>
> I exist to _____.

After a few minutes of thinking and writing, I give them the opportunity to share their answers.

What have I heard consistently over the years? Answers like these:

- "I exist to be a good dad (or mom) and to give my children better opportunities than I had."
- "I exist to help women break free from abusive relationships."
- "I exist to make a positive contribution to society through my work."
- "I exist to glorify God in all that I do."
- "I exist to love people wherever I am."

On the one hand, I am impressed by the sincerity and intensity of their answers. Most people try to live by the values they profess, values that have been shaped over the course of their lives.

On the other, their answers often seem fragmented—a good idea here, a good idea there. More troubling is that many of them (even those at Christian universities) make no mention of loving God the Father, which Jesus says "is the greatest and most important command" (Matt. 22:37–38).

I also wonder why more Christians do not mention Jesus's Great Commission, specifically to "make disciples [followers of Jesus] of all nations" (Matt. 28:18–20; see Mark 13:10; Luke 24:44–49; John 20:21, 31; Acts 1:8). Hardly anyone refers to these passages, even though they clarify our mission in life—what Jesus sends us to do.

As they take turns sharing, I want to wrap my arms around their answers and pull them together in a way that simultaneously honors God, attends to God's teaching in the Bible, and makes sense of our lives where we all live—with feet on the ground and paddles in the water.

I then share the framework by which I try to live my life, which I summarize in six affirmations.

Our Identity

(1) "We are Christians."

Our Character

(2) "We are growing into the likeness of Jesus."

Our Immediate Purpose: Service

(3) "We serve those in need."

Our Penultimate[17] Purposes: Evangelism and Discipleship

(4) "We help non-Christians to know God through Jesus Christ."

and

(5) "We help Christians to know God better through Jesus Christ."

Our Ultimate Purpose: God-centeredness

(6) "We center our lives on God."

I frame these ideas in terms of who *we* are and what *we* must do together as Christians, not merely who we are as individuals. The apostle Paul, for example, thanked God for the Philippians' partnership in advancing the gospel (Phil. 1:3–5), which is the good news that Jesus died and rose again (1 Cor. 15:1–4).

Those six categories and affirmations are my best attempt to summarize the Bible's teaching on our position and calling before God.

---

[17] *Penultimate* means "next to last in a list or series." God-centeredness (such as worshiping God) is our *ultimate* purpose.

To clarify:

- **Our identity** is that we are Christians—followers of Jesus Christ. We are individuals who have been adopted, declared righteous, set apart, made alive, and chosen *by God himself*. That is how God sees us and how we should see ourselves.

- **Our character** is being conformed to the character of Jesus as we cooperate with the work of the Holy Spirit.

- **Our immediate purpose** is to serve others with our time, talents, and resources. We do so because we value those in need, whether they are Christians or not.

- **Our penultimate purposes** are both to help people know God for the first time through Jesus (which is evangelism) and to help people know God better through Jesus (which is discipleship)—all by the power of the Holy Spirit. More specifically, we make disciples of Jesus by going to others (as opposed to waiting for them to come to us), by proclaiming and explaining the good news that Jesus died and rose from the dead to bring people to God, and by calling them to turn from sin and trust in Jesus. We baptize new believers and teach them to obey all that Jesus commanded. That is Jesus's Great Commission; that is the church's mission, what we will do until he returns. And this mission connects to our value system: because we value non-Christians, we evangelize; because we value Christians, we disciple.

- **Our ultimate purpose** is to center our lives on God, particularly as we love, worship, and glorify him above all. We do so because we value God above all. All of life (including pursuing Christlike character, serving others, and making disciples of Jesus) can be and should be an act of worship.

Viewed together, these parts create a life framework we can carry with us into each of our life settings—in our families, in our churches, in our communities, in our vocations, and throughout the world. I summarize this information on the following page.

A Christian Life Framework

Our Identity	Our Character	Our Immediate Purpose	Our Penultimate Purposes	Our Ultimate Purpose
We are Christians.	We are growing into the likeness of Jesus.	We serve.	We evangelize. We disciple.	We center our lives on God.

Unified Purposes and Diverse Lives in the Body of Christ

As Christians, we do not have the right to determine the central purposes of the Christian life. That is something God has already determined and communicated to us.

In this book, you will study God's purposes for our lives as outlined in Scripture. My hope is that if someone asks you why you exist, passages like these will shape your response:

- Matthew 22:37–40; 28:18–20
- Mark 13:10
- Luke 24:44–49
- John 4:23–24; 20:21
- Acts 1:8
- 1 Corinthians 10:31
- 1 Peter 4:10–11

These same passages will also help you clarify for others why they exist, as you pass this information along to them.

For example, in Matthew 28:18–20, Jesus said to his disciples:

> "All authority has been given to me in heaven and on earth. Go, therefore, and make disciples of all nations, baptizing them in the name of the Father and of the Son and of the Holy Spirit, teaching them to observe everything I have commanded you. And remember, I am with you always, to the end of the age."

Having received authority from God the Father (v. 18), Jesus dictates our mission in life: to make disciples, or followers, of himself (vv. 19–20).

And in Acts 1:8, Jesus said:

> "But you will receive power when the Holy Spirit has come on you, and you will be my witnesses in Jerusalem, in all Judea and Samaria, and to the end of the earth."

There we learn that the Holy Spirit would empower the disciples to witness to Jesus, particularly to his sacrificial, sin-atoning death and victorious, life-giving resurrection (Acts 3:15). In doing so,

Jesus clarifies our source of power and what we must proclaim to the world.

In these ways, submitting ourselves to God's purposes for our lives is one of the hallmarks of the Christian life. We do so by submitting to Jesus, through the Holy Spirit, as outlined in the Bible.

While we share the same overarching purposes for our lives, certainly there is God-honoring diversity in the body of Christ. We have different spiritual gifts, talents, abilities, experiences, and callings. For example, the Holy Spirit apportions spiritual gifts "to each person as he wills" (1 Cor. 12:11).

And regarding our life settings, we live our lives as God assigns, whether we are single or married, with children or without, in this place or that. These are the diverse contexts in which we pursue God's purposes.

While I do not believe that people need to choose my exact wording as reflected on the previous pages, God calls us as the church to serve, to evangelize, and to disciple—all for the love, worship, and glory of God. Though our contribution to advancing God's purposes will differ, we share these purposes in common.

The Benefits of Having a Clear Life Framework

Before we begin our study, in what areas of our lives will we benefit if we have a clear life framework?

1. **Time:** A clear life framework will help us to spend our time on what matters most and to avoid wasting time on things of no significance.
2. **Money:** A clear life framework will help us to give, to spend, and to save our money in ways that align with God's purposes.
3. **Talents:** A clear life framework will help us to use our spiritual gifts, natural talents, and learned abilities for the glory of God and not for selfish interests.
4. **Partnership:** A clear life framework will help us to partner with like-minded individuals who share the same value system,

whether we are seeking a marriage partner or selecting and serving within a local church.
5. **Prayer:** A clear life framework will help us to consider how we pray—for God to work in us, through us, and for his glory.
6. **Temptation:** A clear life framework will help us to resist temptation and to repent of our sins, particularly as we fight for the truth that God is our highest value and our greatest joy, not the temporary, God-dishonoring pleasures of sin.
7. **Preparation:** A clear life framework will help us to prepare to give an account of our lives to God, as we pursue his priorities for our lives even now.

Everything we desire, value, think, say, and do will benefit if we know the main purposes God wants us to pursue.

This Book

Given that this book covers a wide range of topics, it is not a step-by-step guide on how to identify your spiritual gifts or how to share your faith. However, it does outline how we can begin to think about these broad topics and how they fit together.

This book highlights the roles that each member of the Trinity plays in establishing our position before God and in shaping the direction for our lives, particularly in units one, six, and seven. Without minimizing the unity of God, this book points out the distinctive work of each member of the Trinity in our lives. Once you see how the biblical authors draw our attention to this, the way you read the Bible and teach it to others will never be the same.

If you are unsure whether you are in a personal relationship with God or where you will spend eternity, please read "The Path to God" on my website at JaySimala.com.

For Reflection and Discussion

Use these pages to respond to the following questions, to record your prayers to God, and/or to prepare to process this information with others.

1. Before reading this chapter, how would you have completed this sentence: "I exist to _____"?
2. What parts of this chapter were the most helpful or the most challenging to you? Why?
3. What interferes with you having a clear sense of direction for your life?
4. What are your motivations for reading this book?
5. Whether it is a church leader or one or more friends, with whom do you plan to study this book?

Notes

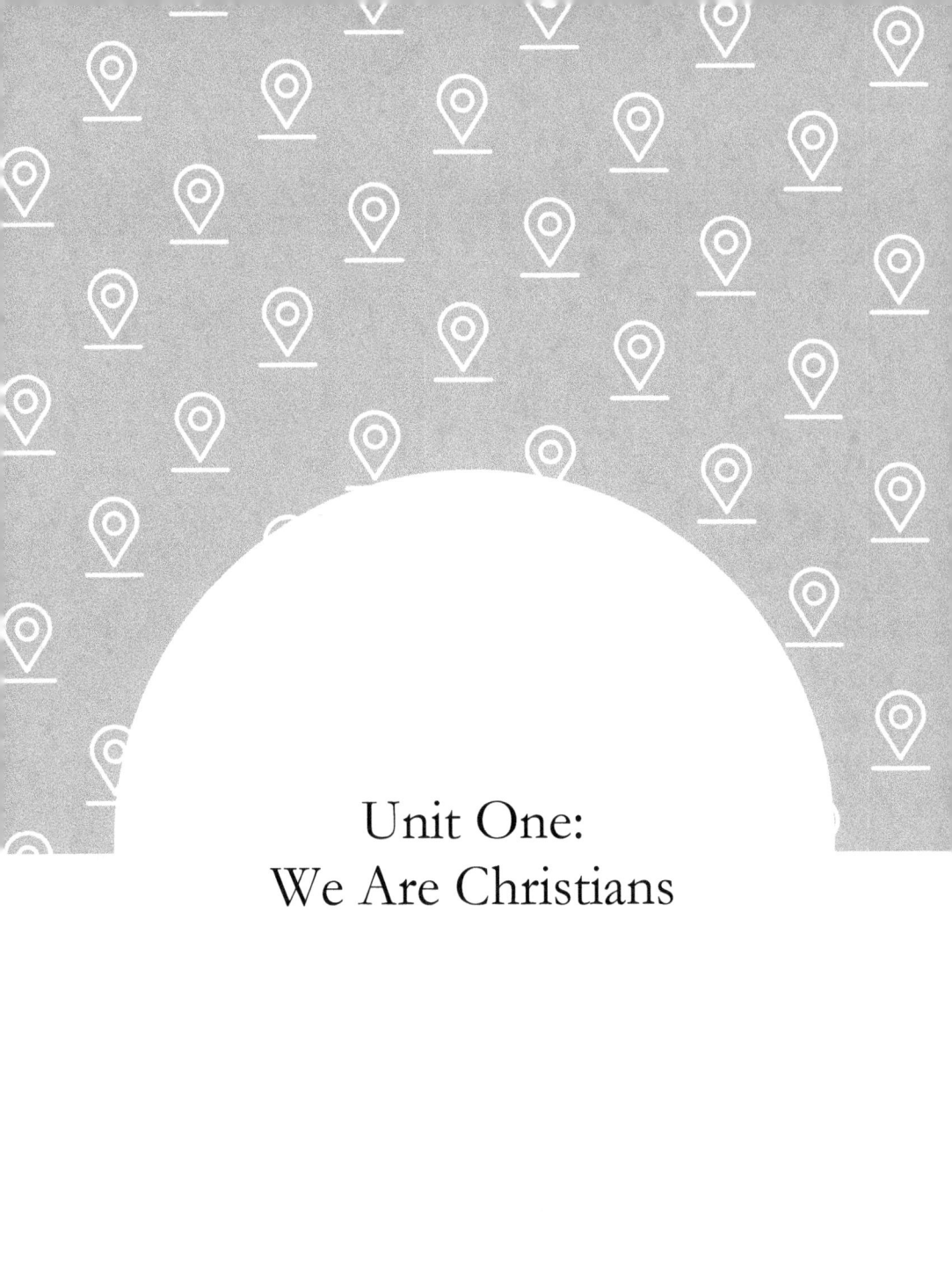

Unit One:
We Are Christians

Overview

Introduction

Once someone becomes a Christian, I want to celebrate out loud what God himself has done:

> "Praise God! You are now his child, and he is your Father. He has declared you righteous in his sight based on the perfect life, death, and resurrection of his Son. You have already been set apart for God and his purposes, and he will help you grow in holiness. At one time you were dead in your sins, but he made you alive through his Word and by his Spirit, both of which enabled you to believe. And he set his affection on you long ago, even before he created the universe. It is a joy to be your brother in Christ!"

Embedded within that paragraph are five great truths that we will explore in this unit: for all who are Christians, in Christ and by the power of the Holy Spirit, God has (1) adopted us, (2) declared us righteous, (3) set us apart, (4) made us alive, and (5) chosen us.

This unit explores the question, "What is true of the Christian from God's perspective?"

Reading

Read lessons one through five.

Memory Verses[18]

- "And because you are sons, God sent the Spirit of his Son into our hearts, crying, '*Abba*, Father!'" (Gal. 4:6)
- "And some of you used to be like this. But you were washed, you were sanctified, you were justified in the name of the Lord Jesus Christ and by the Spirit of our God." (1 Cor. 6:11)

---

[18] All the memory passages are taken from the *Christian Standard Bible* (*CSB*). If you choose to do so, memorize these verses in your preferred version.

1. Adopted

As both a joy and a privilege, my wife and I sponsor children from around the world. A small amount of money goes a long way toward providing food and clothes for a child and toward paying for school fees. Early in our marriage, we took our commitment a step further: we adopted a boy from Ethiopia, a boy who has grown into a young man. Our primary motivation in both sponsoring children and adopting is theological: God loved us by adopting us into his family, so we want to show love to those in need. By God's grace "we love because he first loved us" (1 John 4:19), which is true for all Christians.

While God created all people and provides for them regardless of their beliefs (Matt. 5:45; Acts 14:17), no one enters this world as part of his spiritual family. Because of our disposition to sin and repeatedly choosing to sin, we are alienated from God and subject to wrath (Rom. 5:10; Eph. 2:3). But God's love triumphs over both our sin nature and our ongoing resistance: "See what great love the Father has given us that we should be called God's children—and we are!" (1 John 3:1).

This is the doctrine of *adoption*, which is the act by which God brings someone into his family. How does this happen?

1. We were adopted by God the Father.

> He predestined us to be adopted as sons through Jesus Christ for himself, according to the good pleasure of his will. (Eph. 1:5)

God adopts people into his family, and it has always been this way. Though there was nothing inherently superior about the Israelites, God set his affection on them and chose them as his son, his child (Ex. 4:22; Rom. 9:4). This did not mean that each individual Israelite was in a right, reconciled relationship with him (Rom. 2:28–29; 9:6–8). Both then and now, God adopts individuals to be in his spiritual family, for all who have faith in him, both Jews and non-Jews alike (Rom. 4:13–17; Gal. 3:25–29). God "predestined us to be adopted," which was the result of his love and his will (Eph. 1:4–5). God is the one who initiates toward us, even from eternity past.

2. We were adopted through the work of Jesus Christ.

> When the time came to completion, God sent his Son, born of a woman, born under the law, to redeem those under the law, so that we might receive adoption as sons. (Gal. 4:4–5)

Prior to becoming a Christian, each of us was a slave to sin, owing a debt to God that we could not afford to pay (John 8:34). Put simply, we needed to be redeemed. God sent his Son to the cross to pay our debt to God himself, to secure our forgiveness, and to set us free from slavery to sin (John 8:36; Eph. 1:7; Col. 2:13–14). All of this was necessary for us to receive adoption into God's family (John 1:12; Gal. 4:4–5).

3. We experience adoption by the Holy Spirit.

> And because you are sons, God sent the Spirit of his Son into our hearts, crying, "*Abba*, Father!" (Gal. 4:6)

When babies are born into this world, they immediately cry out—for breath, for comfort, for life. When God adopts us into his family, we cry out to him by the very Holy Spirit he provides—for "*Abba*, Father!" Both terms emphasize our intimacy with God and access to him, all made possible by the Holy Spirit (Rom. 8:15–16; Gal. 4:6).

Life with God

What, then, is true of us who are now adopted? We are not obligated or bound to live according to our sinful tendencies, but we are led by the Holy Spirit (Rom. 8:12–14). And because we are God's children, we do not fear (Rom. 8:15). Instead, we cry out to God as our Father and rest in the assurance that we are his children (Rom. 8:15–16; Heb. 12:5–11). "And if children, also heirs—heirs of God and coheirs with Christ—if indeed we suffer with him so that we may also be glorified with him" (Rom. 8:17). Together, we eagerly anticipate our final adoption—the final redemption of our bodies in heaven (Rom. 8:23).

For Reflection and Discussion

Use these two pages to respond to the following questions, to record your prayers to God, and/or to prepare to process this information with others.

1. How would you explain the concept of spiritual adoption in your own words?
2. Describe your life prior to God adopting you into his family. What was it like to be Father-less in various areas of your life?
3. What are some of the joys of relating to God as your Father? What are some of the responsibilities?

2. Declared Righteous

Apart from trusting in Jesus Christ, all of us would stand condemned in the presence of God the Father. Why? God is righteous (Ps. 11:7), and each of us is unrighteous (Rom. 3:10), in that we fall short of God's perfect moral standard (Rom. 3:23). And because God is just (Deut. 32:4), he will certainly judge those who are unrighteous (Ps. 7:11).

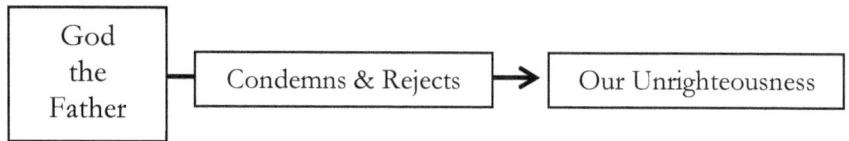

At this point, there are only two options. Either we will suffer under God's judgment because we are unrighteous (Rom. 2:8; 6:23) or we will be declared righteous by God, despite the fact that we are not righteous in and of ourselves. That is precisely what God does for those who trust in him:

> But to the one who does not work, but believes on him who declares the ungodly to be righteous, his faith is credited for righteousness. (Rom. 4:5)

This is the doctrine of *justification*, which is the legal act by which God declares unrighteous people to be righteous in his sight, even though they are not righteous in and of themselves. How does this work?

1. We were declared righteous by God the Father.

> God presented him to demonstrate his righteousness at the present time, so that he would be righteous and declare righteous the one who has faith in Jesus. (Rom. 3:26; see 1 John 1:9)

In the act of justification, God does not transform someone into a righteous person in his or her thoughts, words, and actions; that is the process called *progressive sanctification*. Instead, God *declares* a person righteous in his sight; he pronounces the unrighteous person to be righteous. Because we cannot meet this standard on our own, it must come from someone else, from Jesus.

2. We were declared righteous by the work of Jesus Christ.

> He [God the Father] made the one who did not know sin [Jesus] to be sin for us, so that in him [Jesus] we might become the righteousness of God. (2 Cor. 5:21; see 1 Pet. 3:18)

Although no mere human being is righteous (Rom. 3:10), Jesus is the Righteous One who never sinned (Acts 3:14; 1 Pet. 2:22). And so begins the great exchange for all who trust in Jesus (2 Cor. 5:21). Based on how Jesus's death satisfied God's justice, God credits our unrighteousness to Jesus (even though he is perfectly righteous). And based on Jesus's perfect obedience to God, God credits Jesus's righteousness to us (even though we are not righteous). Jesus and Jesus alone earned and secured our right standing before God.

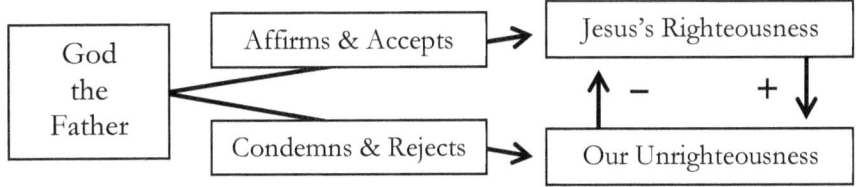

3. We were declared righteous by the work of the Spirit.

> You were justified in the name of the Lord Jesus Christ and by the Spirit of our God. (1 Cor. 6:11)

One of the many works of the Holy Spirit is to apply God's declaration to our lives—to make justification a reality.

Life with God

We will never be perfect in this life, but we are now at peace with God by faith in Jesus Christ, not by works (Rom. 5:1). We "are justified freely by his grace" (Rom. 3:24), so we receive that gift from God with joy and gratitude. By the Spirit, we then strive to live a righteous, godly life (Rom. 14:17). And though we will always fall short in this life, our final, moral transformation awaits us when we are with Jesus in heaven (1 John 3:2).

For Reflection and Discussion

Use these two pages to respond to the following questions, to record your prayers to God, and/or to prepare to process this information with others.

1. Read Romans 3:9–20. What does it mean that each of us is unrighteous? In your life, what are some examples of unrighteous thoughts, words, and/or actions?
2. What does it mean that Jesus is perfectly righteous? What are some examples of how Jesus obeyed God perfectly while on earth? How did that uniquely qualify him to stand in our place at the cross?
3. How would you explain justification in your own words? Can someone earn justification? Why or why not?

3. Set Apart

Before turning to Jesus in faith, each of us was part of a mass of people who were living apart from God. Put differently, we were part of the *world*, which is the global community of those who oppose God, those who refuse to worship and follow him (John 3:19; see Ps. 2:1–3).

But when we turned from our sins and trusted in Jesus, God not only adopted us into his family (Gal. 4:4–7) and declared us righteous (Rom. 3:21–26) but he also set us apart or *sanctified* us:

> But we ought to thank God always for you, brothers and sisters loved by the Lord, because from the beginning God has chosen you for salvation *through sanctification by the Spirit* and through belief in the truth. (2 Thess. 2:13, emphasis mine)

This is the doctrine of *sanctification*.

First and foremost, sanctification is *the act by which God sets people apart for himself and his purposes, based on Jesus and his work*. In that sense of the word, at conversion Christians are 100% set apart (100% sanctified) because they are 100% forgiven because of Jesus's death and resurrection. In this way all Christians are "saints" or "holy ones"—those who have been completely set apart for God and his purposes. There is another sense of sanctification. It is *the process by which we become progressively transformed into the likeness of Jesus Christ* (1 Thess. 4:3). Over time, we grow in holiness and learn to resist temptations.[19] What do we know about this doctrine?

1. We were set apart by God the Father.

> To all who are in Rome, loved by God, called as saints. Grace to you and peace from God our Father and the Lord Jesus Christ. (Rom. 1:7)

God is the one who initiates with love toward his people and calls them to himself (Rom. 1:7; 1 John 4:19). This call is not a mere invitation; instead, this call accomplishes God's own will,

---

[19] See David Peterson's book, *Possessed by God*.

effectively drawing people to himself (John 6:44; Rom. 8:30). And this call immediately results in the creation of "saints"—those who are set apart or sanctified by God and for God.

2. We were set apart by Jesus Christ.

- "And some of you used to be like this. But you were washed, you were sanctified, you were justified in the name of the Lord Jesus Christ and by the Spirit of our God." (1 Cor. 6:11)
- "By this will, we have been sanctified through the offering of the body of Jesus Christ once for all time." (Heb. 10:10)

The name of Jesus means "Yahweh saves" or "Yahweh is salvation." And by that name God set us apart (1 Cor. 6:11). Through his death and resurrection, Jesus completed the work that secured our right standing before God (1 Cor. 1:30; Heb. 10:10).

3. We were set apart by the Holy Spirit.

Peter, an apostle of Jesus Christ: To those chosen, living as exiles…chosen according to the foreknowledge of God the Father, through the sanctifying work of the Spirit, to be obedient and to be sprinkled with the blood of Jesus Christ. May grace and peace be multiplied to you. (1 Pet. 1:1–2)

At the moment of our conversion, the Holy Spirit completely set us apart for God and his purposes (1 Pet. 1:2). From this perspective, we are already sanctified, set in place for God to use us by the power of the Holy Spirit.

Life with God

In light of the truth that God has already set us apart for himself and his purposes, how shall we live? With God's help, we seek moral transformation (or *progressive sanctification*). For example, we strive for sexual purity in our thoughts and actions (Matt. 5:27–30; 1 Thess. 4:3). The primary means by which God purifies us is by the truth of his Word (John 17:17), and so we turn to the Bible again and again for guidance. As we continue in the Christian faith, the end result is eternal life (Rom. 6:22).

For Reflection and Discussion

Use these two pages to respond to the following questions, to record your prayers to God, and/or to prepare to process this information with others.

1. What does it mean that non-Christians are part of the world? See, for example, John 3:19–20 and 1 John 2:15–17.
2. What does it mean that you are now set apart? In other words, set apart from what? By whom? To what?
3. How should you live now that you have been set apart? What are some areas of your life where you want to live more righteously? Explain.

4. Alive

We know death when we see it: there is no animation, no responsiveness, no life. Death surrounds us in this life, and it takes different forms.[20]

There is *physical death*, which results from natural causes, tragic accidents, and murder. But much worse is *spiritual death*, which is the state in which people live apart from God.

Paul described his readers prior to becoming Christians in this way: "You were dead in your trespasses and sins" (Eph. 2:1). To be "dead" in that sense of the word is to be unresponsive to God, disconnected from God, and under the judgment of God (Rom. 1:18; 6:23; 7:5), whether in this life or the next (Rom. 8:6; Rev. 21:8).

In that spiritual state, we lack both the ability and the desire to turn to God. So, in his mercy and love, God performs a miracle to bring us to life:

> But God, who is rich in mercy, because of his great love that he had for us, made us alive with Christ even though we were dead in trespasses. You are saved by grace! (Eph. 2:4–5)

This is the doctrine of *regeneration*, which is the act by which God overcomes our spiritual death and makes us alive to himself. How, more specifically, do we come to life?

1. We were brought to life by God the Father.

> But to all who did receive him, he gave them the right to be children of God, to those who believe in his name, who were born, not of natural descent, or of the will of the flesh, or of the will of man, but of God. (John 1:12–13)

God initiates and brings his people to life, for those who are dead to God do not come to life on their own.[21] Just as Jesus raised Lazarus from the dead in the physical realm (John 11:38–44), God

---

[20] See Lesson 14 in my book *Start*.
[21] Nor do spiritually-enslaved people set themselves free (Rom. 8:2) or spiritually-blind people give themselves sight (2 Cor. 4:6).

brings his people to life in the spiritual realm (Eph. 2:4–5; Col. 2:13–14). Our spiritual birth did not come from any human desire or decision but from God (John 1:13).

2. We were brought to life with Jesus Christ.

> And when you were dead in trespasses and in the uncircumcision of your flesh, he made you alive with him and forgave us all our trespasses. (Col. 2:13)

God brought us to life with Jesus, the one who died for our sins and whom God raised from the dead (Col. 2:12–14; Eph. 2:5). God then continues to use his power on behalf of his people (Eph. 1:19–20).

3. We were brought to life by the Holy Spirit and the Word.

- "He saved us—not by works of righteousness that we had done, but according to his mercy—through the washing of regeneration and renewal by the Holy Spirit." (Tit. 3:5)
- "Because you have been born again—not of perishable seed but of imperishable—through the living and enduring word of God." (1 Pet. 1:23)

The Holy Spirit regenerates us, bringing us to life (Tit. 3:5; John 6:63). We are born again, or born from above, by his work (John 3:3–8). And the Holy Spirit's activity is coupled with the Word of God to accomplish this work in us (1 Pet. 1:23; James 1:18; Acts 10:44). We then have the ability to live out this resurrection life, both now and into eternity (Rom. 6:4–5; 8:11).

Life with God

When we were born into this world, the first thing we did was breathe. And when God made us alive to himself, the first thing we did was turn from our sin and trust in Jesus (1 John 5:1). While the transformation of our character is not immediate, we practice righteous living (1 John 2:29), and we love our Christian brothers and sisters (1 John 4:7). This is some of the evidence of God's supernatural work in our lives—evidence of new, eternal life. Conversely, all those who are living in persistent, unrepentant sin demonstrate that they are not born again (1 John 3:4–10).

For Reflection and Discussion

Use these two pages to respond to the following questions, to record your prayers to God, and/or to prepare to process this information with others.

1. How would you have described yourself prior to becoming a Christian? In what ways were you spiritually dead?
2. When you became a Christian, in what ways did it feel like you came alive to God? For example, how did you begin to think differently? How did your desires and values change?
3. What are some of the implications for our lives now that we are alive to God? In other words, how does a person die to sin (and the old way of life) and live for God?

5. Chosen

How has God blessed you? When I ask people this question, the majority of people focus on blessings such as food, shelter, health, family, and friends. Each of these is indeed a blessing from God (Matt. 5:45; James 1:17). But there is a deeper, eternal set of blessings from God—blessings that no one can take away from Christians. The apostle Paul praised God accordingly:

> Blessed is the God and Father of our Lord Jesus Christ, who has blessed us with every spiritual blessing in the heavens in Christ. For he chose us in him, before the foundation of the world, to be holy and blameless in love before him. (Eph. 1:3–4)

God "has blessed us with every spiritual blessing in the heavens in Christ" (v. 3). Ephesians 1:4–14 outlines these blessings, which include God's adopting us into his family and forgiving our sins.[22]

The first blessing Paul lists is found in verse 4: "for he [God the Father] chose us." Christians refer to this as the doctrine of *election*, which is the "act of God before creation in which he chooses some people to be saved, not on account of any foreseen merit in them, but only because of his sovereign good pleasure."[23] What do we know about this doctrine?

1. We were chosen by God the Father.

- "He predestined us to be adopted as sons through Jesus Christ for himself, according to the good pleasure of his will." (Eph. 1:5)
- "For those he foreknew he also predestined to be conformed to the image of his Son, so that he would be the firstborn among many brothers and sisters." (Rom. 8:29)

If you are a Christian, God set his affection on you, choosing you from eternity past (Eph. 1:4–5). The Bible's language in this regard is diverse: God *chose* us (Eph. 1:4), God *foreknew* and *predestined* us (Rom. 8:29; 1 Pet. 1:2), and God *appointed* us to

---

[22] *NIV Biblical Theology Study Bible* (hereafter *NIV BTSB*), 2,117.
[23] Grudem, *Christian Beliefs*, 79.

eternal life (Acts 13:48). God is the one who freely chose us, who set his affection on us, and who initiated the relationship (Rom. 9:15; 1 John 4:19). And he did this so that we would "be conformed to the image of his Son" (Rom. 8:29), beginning in this life but ultimately realized in the life to come.

2. We were chosen in Christ.

> For he chose us in him [Jesus], before the foundation of the world, to be holy and blameless in love before him. (Eph. 1:4)

God's eternal choice was made "in him," for Jesus is the one through whom (and in whom) God made his choice. In other words, Jesus is God's personal agent of this blessing. And God granted this grace "in him, before the foundation of the world" (Eph. 1:4; see 2 Tim. 1:9).

3. We were chosen by the Holy Spirit.

> But we ought to thank God always for you, brothers and sisters loved by the Lord, because from the beginning God has chosen you for salvation *through sanctification by the Spirit* and through belief in the truth. (2 Thess. 2:13, emphasis mine)

The Holy Spirit brings God the Father's choice into reality or actualizes his choice. At conversion, Christians are *completely set apart or sanctified in their position before God* by the Spirit of God and by believing in Jesus Christ (1 Thess. 1:4–5; 2 Thess. 2:13). And over time, Christians become *increasingly holy or progressively sanctified in their moral development before God* (1 Thess. 4:3). In these ways and more, the Holy Spirit completes the work of the Father and the Son, including their act of choosing us for eternal life.

Life with God

God's choice took place in eternity past, but we experience salvation when we turn from our sin and trust in Jesus (Acts 20:21). Then, we confirm our calling and election in concrete ways, particularly as we demonstrate godly character (Rom. 8:29; Col. 3:12–17; 2 Pet. 1:10). Election is a mysterious, awe-inspiring reality, and it results in worship as we praise God's glorious grace (Eph. 1:6, 12, 14).

For Reflection and Discussion

Use these two pages to respond to the following questions, to record your prayers to God, and/or to prepare to process this information with others.

1. If you have turned from sin and trusted in Jesus, how do you respond to the truth that God chose you before the foundation of the world?
2. What aspects of election are comforting? What aspects are confusing?
3. How should you live in light of God's electing love? Put differently, how should you respond to God's loving, eternal initiation?

Guide for Meeting with Others

Open with Prayer

Recite Memory Verses

For Discussion

1. Before Becoming a Christian

   a. Identify at least three words to describe your life apart from Jesus Christ. Explain each word in detail.
   b. Read Ephesians 2:1–3. How does Paul describe our lives prior to becoming Christians? Identify and explain these challenges.
   c. Read 1 Corinthians 6:9–10. Explain the apostle Paul's main point. Then, for each group of people he identifies (such as "sexually immoral people" or "idolaters"), describe the group in your own words.

2. After Becoming a Christian

   a. Read 1 Corinthians 6:11. Identify and explain what is now true of all Christians.
   b. Read Ephesians 1:3–14. Verse by verse, identify the many blessings of God in the life of a Christian.

3. Responding to God

   a. What part of the lessons on the preceding pages did you find to be the most helpful or challenging? Why?
   b. Name one or more of your desires that you want to bring to God in prayer (for yourself and/or for others).

Pray for One Another

Notes

Notes

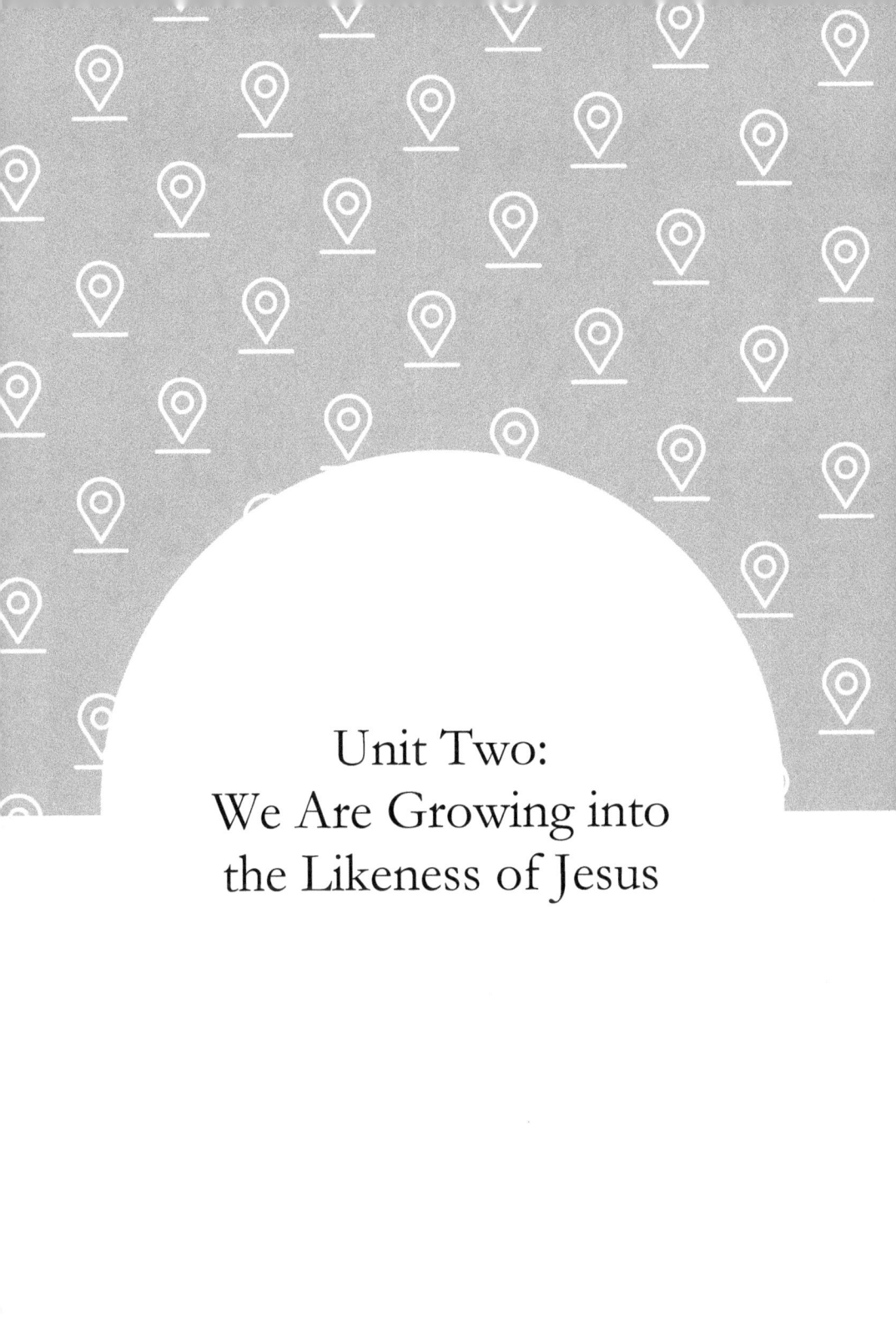

Unit Two:
We Are Growing into the Likeness of Jesus

Overview

Introduction

For all who are Christians, God's will is that we become "conformed to the image of his Son" (Rom. 8:29). Put simply, he wants us to be more like Jesus, not simply in our words and actions but also in our character. This transformation of our character includes the way we think, what we desire, and what we value.

And while there are many things in life that are out of our control, our character is not. Regardless of the trials we face or the way people treat us, we can choose faith, hope, love, and personal holiness, imitating our Savior with the strength God provides.

This unit explores the question, "How should we pursue the character transformation that God desires?"

Reading

Read lessons six through ten.

Memory Verses

- "So if you have been raised with Christ, seek the things above, where Christ is, seated at the right hand of God. Set your minds on things above, not on earthly things." (Col. 3:1–2)
- "But the fruit of the Spirit is love, joy, peace, patience, kindness, goodness, faithfulness, gentleness, and self-control. The law is not against such things." (Gal. 5:22–23)

6. Stand Strong through Your Trials

Trials take many forms, such as relational conflicts, financial pressures, and physical challenges, and each of them tests our faith. Regardless of the nature of the trial, we all have a choice.

We can either stand strong under the weight of the burden by choosing God and the strength he offers. Or we will collapse under (or run from) the weight by choosing self-centered strategies for managing or escaping the emotional pain.

While trials are unavoidable in this life, what are some of the primary responses that please God and develop our character?

1. We choose joy.

> Consider it a great joy, my brothers and sisters, whenever you experience various trials, because you know that the testing of your faith produces endurance. And let endurance have its full effect, so that you may be mature and complete, lacking nothing. (James 1:2–4)

We experience joy in God himself (Ps. 32:11), in his Word (Ps. 119:16), and in his work in others' lives (Phil. 1:3–5). While trials often lead to other reactions (like sadness and frustration), we also view them as opportunities to rejoice, precisely because God uses our trials to shape our character (James 1:2). As God tests and refines our faith through trials, we grow in endurance, which is the ability to stand strong under the burdens of this life (v. 3). As this character quality grows, it leads us to mature more fully, "lacking nothing" (v. 4).

2. We ask for wisdom.

> Now if any of you lacks wisdom, he should ask God—who gives to all generously and ungrudgingly—and it will be given to him. But let him ask in faith without doubting. For the doubter is like the surging sea, driven and tossed by the wind. That person should not expect to receive anything from the Lord, being double-minded and unstable in all his ways. (James 1:5–8)

Wisdom is knowledge from God that is applied skillfully to specific situations, whether to govern (Ezra 7:25), to live a life of moral purity (Prov. 5:1), or to teach others about Jesus (Col. 1:28). God promises to grant us the wisdom and skill to stand strong under trials (James 1:5), if only we ask with a consistent, even faith, not like a wave that is driven up, down, and around by the wind (vv. 6–8).

3. We hope in God.

> Let the brother of humble circumstances boast in his exaltation, but let the rich boast in his humiliation because he will pass away like a flower of the field. For the sun rises and, together with the scorching wind, dries up the grass; its flower falls off, and its beautiful appearance perishes. In the same way, the rich person will wither away while pursuing his activities. Blessed is the one who endures trials, because when he has stood the test he will receive the crown of life that God has promised to those who love him. (James 1:9–12)

Hope is looking to God and the future he guarantees. Whether we are lowly in status or wealthy and well-known, God calls us to take our eyes off this world and its pursuits (vv. 9–11). Ultimately, we boast not in our circumstances but in God and Jesus Christ (Jer. 9:23–24; 1 Cor. 1:30–31). All who endure trials are blessed indeed, for God will grant them eternal life (James 1:12).

Life with God

Godly character is a choice. Through the strength Jesus offers (2 Cor. 12:9), we have the ability to choose God and his ways in the midst of trials, such as choosing joy, wisdom, hope, or any other character attribute. The alternative is to ignore God and his will for our lives, such as turning to addictions, despair, or any other self-centered response to drown out the pain. God grants us the ability to choose wisely as we look forward to the crown of eternal life. But the first step is to acknowledge that we are in the midst of a trial and then to cry out to God for help. He delights in helping us do what we cannot do on our own.

For Reflection and Discussion

Use these two pages to respond to the following questions, to record your prayers to God, and/or to prepare to process this information with others.

1. What are some of the trials you are currently facing? What makes them so difficult for you and for those you love?
2. How are you tempted to manage your trials in sinful ways? For example, are you tempted to medicate your emotional pain? How so?
3. How is God shaping your character through your trials? How might he use you to help others in similar circumstances?

7. Run with Endurance

The Bible uses a variety of word pictures to describe our relationship with Jesus. We are sheep following the Good Shepherd (John 10:3, 11). We are ambassadors for Christ (2 Cor. 5:20; Eph. 6:20). We are a bride to Jesus, the Lamb of God (Rev. 19:7; 21:9). And we are also runners in a race—a race that God calls us to "run with endurance" (Heb. 12:1). How do we run to cross the finish line?

1. We resist sin by looking to Jesus.

> Therefore, since we also have such a large cloud of witnesses surrounding us, let us lay aside every hindrance and the sin that so easily ensnares us. Let us run with endurance the race that lies before us, keeping our eyes on Jesus, the source and perfecter of our faith. For the joy that lay before him, he endured the cross, despising the shame, and sat down at the right hand of the throne of God. For consider him who endured such hostility from sinners against himself, so that you won't grow weary and give up. In struggling against sin, you have not yet resisted to the point of shedding your blood. (Heb. 12:1–4)

The witnesses of Hebrews 11 modeled the faith that we must imitate (Heb. 12:1; see 11:6). They witnessed to the truth about God and his Word, and they witnessed on his behalf. As we consider their lives, in Hebrews 12 the author encourages us to run this race of life by laying aside obstacles to our faith, particularly our sin (vv. 1, 4). We endure in this race by looking to Jesus, the one who endured the cross to bring us to God (v. 2; 7:27). He is not only our sacrifice but also our model of endurance. Jesus's race—particularly his life, death, and resurrection—is the very ground under Christians' feet (2:9–11).

2. We receive the Lord's discipline.

> And you have forgotten the exhortation that addresses you as sons: My son, do not take the Lord's discipline lightly or lose heart when you are reproved by him, for the Lord disciplines the one he loves and punishes every son he receives. Endure suffering as discipline: God is dealing with you as sons. For what son is there

> that a father does not discipline? But if you are without discipline—which all receive—then you are illegitimate children and not sons. Furthermore, we had human fathers discipline us, and we respected them. Shouldn't we submit even more to the Father of spirits and live? For they disciplined us for a short time based on what seemed good to them, but he does it for our benefit, so that we can share his holiness. No discipline seems enjoyable at the time, but painful. Later on, however, it yields the peaceful fruit of righteousness to those who have been trained by it. (Heb. 12:5–11)

When we trust in Jesus, we become sons and daughters of God the Father (John 1:12; Rom. 8:14–17). And one of God's primary "parental responsibilities" is discipline—the process by which God shapes our character, particularly through our hardships (Heb. 12:5–11). As the perfect Father, God disciplines to demonstrate his love and prove that he has received us, treating us as sons and daughters (vv. 6–9). God disciplines us for our benefit, for it leads to our holiness and righteousness (vv. 10–11).

3. We resolve to endure.

> Therefore, strengthen your tired hands and weakened knees, and make straight paths for your feet, so that what is lame may not be dislocated but healed instead. (Heb. 12:12–13)

Because of the human witnesses that have gone before us, because of Jesus, and because of God's discipline, we resolve to keep running (Heb. 12:12–13). The alternative is to ignore these truths and fall away, particularly when we suffer for our faith.

Life with God

The only way to finish a race is to take the next step—again and again until the end. We do that by listening to and obeying God's Word (Heb. 4:7, 12; 13:22), encouraging one another (10:24–25), and, ultimately, looking to Jesus (12:2). We fall down (or run away from God) when we reject God's Word, avoid fellowship with others, and lose our focus on Jesus. But God is convinced of better things for those who are genuine Christians, "things that are better and that pertain to salvation" (6:9).

For Reflection and Discussion

Use these two pages to respond to the following questions, to record your prayers to God, and/or to prepare to process this information with others.

1. Explain and personalize this word picture: You are a Christian running in a race. From what are you running? To where? With whom? For what reasons do you run? What sins are tripping you up? How would you like to finish your race?
2. Instead of choosing to sin, in what ways should you look to Jesus? What does that look like in practice?
3. How has God disciplined you? What did he teach you in the process?

8. Confirm Your Calling

God declares us righteous by faith based on the life, death, and resurrection of Jesus, which is *justification*.

The apostle Peter writes:

> To those who have received a faith equal to ours *through the righteousness of our God and Savior Jesus Christ*. (2 Pet. 1:1, emphasis mine)

God declares us righteous based on the righteousness of Jesus, who is himself both God and Savior. Then, with the strength God provides through the Holy Spirit, we begin the process of becoming more holy, which is called *sanctification*. Peter then describes both the character God desires and the way to obtain it. What do we know about this process of imitating God?

1. We rely on the power and promises of God.

> His divine power has given us everything required for life and godliness through the knowledge of him who called us by his own glory and goodness. By these he has given us very great and precious promises, so that through them you may share in the divine nature, escaping the corruption that is in the world because of evil desire. (2 Pet. 1:3–4)

Apart from God and his intervention in our lives, we are hopelessly weak and helpless (Rom. 5:6; 8:26). But his power supplies "us everything required for life and godliness" (2 Pet. 1:3). That power comes through a change of perspective: knowing him more fully as the one "who called us by his own glory and goodness" (v. 3). As we cling to God and his promises, we grow into his likeness or "divine nature" (v. 4). Those promises include the gift of the Holy Spirit, "but they also include other promises, such as likeness to God (2 Pet. 1:4; see 1 John 3:2), Christ's return (2 Pet. 3:4), eternal life in heaven (1 Pet. 1:4), and more broadly, all the promises of Scripture that relate to the gift of new life."[24]

---

[24] *ESV Study Bible* (hereafter *ESVSB*), 2,418.

2. We strive to develop godly character.

> For this very reason, make every effort to supplement your faith with goodness, goodness with knowledge, knowledge with self-control, self-control with endurance, endurance with godliness, godliness with brotherly affection, and brotherly affection with love. For if you possess these qualities in increasing measure, they will keep you from being useless or unfruitful in the knowledge of our Lord Jesus Christ. The person who lacks these things is blind and shortsighted and has forgotten the cleansing from his past sins. (2 Pet. 1:5–9)

God provides the power, and yet we must put in the "effort" (v. 5). Peter lists qualities that characterize the maturing Christian (vv. 5–7), which prevent us from being useless and unfruitful in our knowledge of Jesus (v. 8).

3. We confirm our calling and election.

> Therefore, brothers and sisters, make every effort to confirm your calling and election, because if you do these things you will never stumble. For in this way, entry into the eternal kingdom of our Lord and Savior Jesus Christ will be richly provided for you. (2 Pet. 1:10–11)

Practicing these qualities confirms and demonstrates that God called us and chose us (v. 10), paving the way for entrance into the eternal kingdom of Jesus, who is our Lord and Savior (v. 11).

Life with God

God has set his affection on us and promises to finish what he started, including transforming us into the likeness of Jesus (Rom. 8:29; Phil. 1:6; 2 Pet. 1:10). This character transformation requires effort as we make choices that are pleasing to God (Phil. 2:12; 2 Pet. 1:5). And it also requires that we depend on God and the power he supplies, for he is the one who works in and through us (Phil. 2:13; 2 Pet. 1:3–4). In the process, we must keep our focus on God himself—particularly as we study his Word—because godliness comes "through the knowledge of him who called us by his own glory and goodness" (2 Pet. 1:3).

For Reflection and Discussion

Use these two pages to respond to the following questions, to record your prayers to God, and/or to prepare to process this information with others.

1. How does God contribute to your character development (see #1 above)? What are your responsibilities?
2. In light of the list in 2 Peter 1:5–7, evaluate your own character. In particular, in what areas do you need to grow?
3. What would you say to a self-professing Christian who is not maturing in these areas (who shows no signs of growth)?

9. Focus on Jesus Christ

In the book of Colossians, the apostle Paul teaches us how to focus our lives on Jesus Christ. For example, we see and submit to Jesus as the one who is supreme in creation, in the church, and in reconciling us to God the Father (1:15–23). And we walk with Jesus to resist the false teachings of this world (2:4–23). With foundational truths like these in place, how do we pursue a Christ-centered life? Put differently, what does it look like when Jesus is supreme in our lives?

1. We set our minds on heavenly realities.

> So if you have been raised with Christ, seek the things above, where Christ is, seated at the right hand of God. Set your minds on things above, not on earthly things. For you died, and your life is hidden with Christ in God. When Christ, who is your life, appears, then you also will appear with him in glory. (Col. 3:1–4)

All Christians have both died (v. 3) and been raised (v. 1). We have died to God-opposing spiritual forces (2:20) and died to our sin and are now free from its absolute power in our lives (Rom. 6:2, 6, 14).[25] And we have been raised with Christ, made alive by God (Col. 2:13–14), and called to live a new life with God (Rom. 6:4). Therefore, we seek heavenly realities, particularly Christ himself, who rules at the right hand of God (Col. 3:1–2). In time, we will experience the glory of eternal life with Jesus if we persevere in our faith (v. 4; see 1:23).

2. We put to death ungodly character.

> Therefore, put to death what belongs to your earthly nature: sexual immorality, impurity, lust, evil desire, and greed, which is idolatry. Because of these, God's wrath is coming upon the disobedient, and you once walked in these things when you were living in them. But now, put away all the following: anger, wrath, malice, slander, and filthy language from your mouth. Do not lie to one another, since you have put off the old self with its practices. (Col. 3:5–9)

---

[25] *NIVBTSB*, 2,030.

As Christians, we have already died to sin and its power in our lives. But we have to put our sins to death (vv. 5, 8–9), which we do (again and again) until this life is over. We put these sins to death by turning from them and turning to Jesus. These sins belong to our earthly nature (v. 5), which is far from heaven's standard of perfection. Such sins bring God's wrath (v. 6), which is his judgment of sinful people. Christians will still struggle with sin, but, ultimately, such living is a way of the past (v. 7).

3. We put on the character of Jesus.

> And have put on the new self. You are being renewed in knowledge according to the image of your Creator. In Christ there is not Greek and Jew, circumcision and uncircumcision, barbarian, Scythian, slave and free; but Christ is all and in all. Therefore, as God's chosen ones, holy and dearly loved, put on compassion, kindness, humility, gentleness, and patience, bearing with one another and forgiving one another if anyone has a grievance against another. Just as the Lord has forgiven you, so you are also to forgive. Above all, put on love, which is the perfect bond of unity. (Col. 3:10–14)

We put off and we put on: we put off the old self (v. 9) and we put on the new self (v. 10), which is godly character leading to godly actions. This new self is being renewed after the image of Jesus the Creator (v. 10; 1:16), and it is available to all on the basis of faith in Jesus, regardless of one's ethnic or religious background (v. 11). Christians are chosen, holy (or set apart), and beloved by God (v. 12), and therefore we seek to imitate Jesus (vv. 12–14).

Life with God

A changed life begins when we come to God by faith in Christ (Col. 1:3–5, 19–23). To continue in the faith, we put away sin and put on the character of Jesus himself. By God's grace, our character is one of the few things that we can control. God transforms our hearts, which leads to transformed behaviors. For example, Colossians 3:15–17 encourages us to live a God-centered, Christ-centered, Word-centered life—all in the context of Christian community. But none of that will happen if we refuse to turn from our old way of life.

For Reflection and Discussion

Use these two pages to respond to the following questions, to record your prayers to God, and/or to prepare to process this information with others.

1. In light of Colossians 3:5–9, where do you struggle and why?
2. In light of Colossians 3:10–14, where do you most want to grow?
3. In light of Colossians 3:15–17, what concrete steps could you take to be more "God-centered, Christ-centered, Word-centered"?

10. Walk by the Holy Spirit

At the moment we turned from our sins and trusted in Jesus, certain realities became fully realized in our lives. We were 100% forgiven by God (Rom. 4:7; Eph. 1:7), 100% adopted into his family (John 1:12–13; Gal. 4:5), and 100% set apart for him (1 Cor. 6:11; 1 Pet. 1:2).

On this side of heaven, however, the process of becoming more holy (*progressive sanctification*) takes a lifetime, and it is a struggle. But even in the midst of that struggle, we must remember that there is no middle ground: there is only obedience to God or disobedience to God.

In Galatians 5:16–26, the apostle Paul teaches that there are two ways to live: either we live governed by the Holy Spirit or we live in pursuit of our sinful, self-centered desires. How do Christians choose well?

1. We are led by the Holy Spirit.

> I say then, walk by the Spirit and you will certainly not carry out the desire of the flesh. For the flesh desires what is against the Spirit, and the Spirit desires what is against the flesh; these are opposed to each other, so that you don't do what you want. But if you are led by the Spirit, you are not under the law. (Gal. 5:16–18)

Paul instructs us to "walk by the Spirit" (v. 16), which is a word picture that brings together the Holy Spirit's work in our lives and our personal responsibility.[26] The Holy Spirit guides us and empowers us on the Christian path, and yet we are the ones who must choose to walk accordingly.[27] Doing so enables us to avoid gratifying the corrupt desires of our "flesh," which is our corrupt disposition to sin. The desires of the Holy Spirit and those of the flesh are against one another (v. 17). So as we struggle against our sinful desires in this life, we make progress only by the Spirit.

---

[26] Schreiner, *Galatians*, 343.
[27] *ESV SB*, 2,254.

2. We turn from the works of the flesh.

> Now the works of the flesh are obvious: sexual immorality, moral impurity, promiscuity, idolatry, sorcery, hatreds, strife, jealousy, outbursts of anger, selfish ambitions, dissensions, factions, envy, drunkenness, carousing, and anything similar. I am warning you about these things—as I warned you before—that those who practice such things will not inherit the kingdom of God. (Gal. 5:19–21)

The works of the flesh are both obvious and evil, whether they are sexual sins, social/relational sins, or otherwise.[28] Those who consistently live like this will not inherit the kingdom of God (Gal. 5:21; 1 Cor. 6:9–10). Doing so demonstrates a lack of repentance, a lack of trust, and a rejection of God himself.

3. We experience the fruit of the Holy Spirit.

> But the fruit of the Spirit is love, joy, peace, patience, kindness, goodness, faithfulness, gentleness, and self-control. The law is not against such things. Now those who belong to Christ Jesus have crucified the flesh with its passions and desires. (Gal. 5:22–24)

The fruit or manifestation of the Holy Spirit is obvious as well; they are character attributes that impact every area of our lives. While the flesh still has influence over Christians, the flesh has been judged and its power broken (v. 24).[29]

Life with God

When we turn from our sin and turn to God in faith, God breaks the power of sin in our lives (Rom. 6:18, 22) and gives us the Holy Spirit (Acts 10:44; 15:8). While we will continue to sin until we are with Jesus (1 John 3:2), the Holy Spirit empowers us to become more and more like him (Rom. 8:29). And when a Christian sins, "we have an advocate with the Father—Jesus Christ the righteous one. He himself is the atoning sacrifice for our sins, and not only for ours, but also for those of the whole world" (1 John 2:1–2).

---

[28] Schreiner, *Galatians*, 346–348.
[29] Moo, *Galatians*, 368.

For Reflection and Discussion

Use these two pages to respond to the following questions, to record your prayers to God, and/or to prepare to process this information with others.

1. In what ways do you struggle with the list of desires and activities in Galatians 5:19–21? What makes them so appealing to you?
2. In light of the list in Galatians 5:22–23, how would you evaluate your character (whether positively or negatively)? Where, for example, do you see evidence of growth in your life?
3. What practical steps can you take to grow in your character?

Guide for Meeting with Others

Open with Prayer

Recite Memory Verses

For Discussion

1. Walk by the Holy Spirit (from Lesson 10)
   a. Read Galatians 5:16–18 and 5:24–26. Summarize the apostle Paul's teaching in these passages. What, in particular, is the "flesh," and how does it function? How, instead, would you describe the life of a Christian governed by the Spirit?
   b. Read Galatians 5:19–21. In what ways do you struggle with this list of desires and activities? What makes them so appealing?
   c. Read Galatians 5:22–23. In light of this list, how would you evaluate your character? What can you do to participate actively in the Spirit's work? Put differently, what can you do to grow in these character qualities?

2. Character Transformation
   a. Read James 1:2–4, 12. What are some of the trials you are currently facing? How is it possible to choose joy in the midst of your trials?
   b. Read Hebrews 12:1–4. What sins stand between you and God? In what ways do we look to Jesus?
   c. Read 2 Peter 1:3–11. What promises from God are most meaningful to you as you seek to become like Jesus?

3. Responding to God
   a. What part of the lessons on the preceding pages did you find to be the most helpful or challenging? Why?
   b. Name one or more of your desires that you want to bring to God in prayer (for yourself and/or for others).

Pray for One Another

Notes

Notes

Unit Three: We Serve Those in Need

Overview

Introduction

God calls us to be men and women of Christlike character wherever we are, whether in our families, churches, communities, at work, or anywhere else. And in each of these contexts, our most immediate purpose is to serve others, precisely because we value those in need. For example, our children need help with their homework, our churches and missionaries need financial support, and our neighbors need to see and feel the love of Christ.

Ultimately, we do all these things and more to glorify God, for he is the one who has entrusted us with the time, abilities, and resources to help others. In these ways, each of us is a steward of God's resources.

This unit explores the question, "How do we serve others in ways that honor God?"

Reading

Read lessons eleven through fifteen.

Memory Verses

- "For you know the grace of our Lord Jesus Christ: Though he was rich, for your sake he became poor, so that by his poverty you might become rich." (2 Cor. 8:9)
- "If anyone speaks, let it be as one who speaks God's words; if anyone serves, let it be from the strength God provides, so that God may be glorified through Jesus Christ in everything. To him be the glory and the power forever and ever. Amen." (1 Pet. 4:11)

11. Work at Your God-Given Responsibilities

From the beginning, God created humanity to work: "The LORD God took the man and placed him in the garden of Eden to work it and watch over it" (Gen. 2:15). Adam and Eve's sin brought terrible consequences (Gen. 3:8–24), primarily the introduction of both literal and spiritual death into the human race but also the introduction of difficulty in work.

But the call to work remains for all of us. Depending on our age and stage in life, our main responsibilities will change, whether we are working as a student, as a parent, and/or at a full-time or part-time job. But working hard at those main responsibilities is perhaps the most immediate way that we can serve others, serve society, and serve God. In our motivation and attitude and effort, we can glorify God and reflect that he is our ultimate audience (1 Cor. 10:31; Eph. 6:5–9). Despite our sin, how do we honor God in this area of our lives?

1. We imitate.

> Now we command you, brothers and sisters, in the name of our Lord Jesus Christ, to keep away from every brother or sister who is idle and does not live according to the tradition received from us. For you yourselves know how you should imitate us: We were not idle among you; we did not eat anyone's food free of charge; instead, we labored and toiled, working night and day, so that we would not be a burden to any of you. It is not that we don't have the right to support, but we did it to make ourselves an example to you so that you would imitate us. In fact, when we were with you, this is what we commanded you: "If anyone isn't willing to work, he should not eat." (2 Thess. 3:6–10)

The apostle Paul warned the Thessalonians not to associate with self-professing Christians who were idle (v. 6), which is anyone who "isn't willing to work" (v. 10). Even though our life settings are different, Paul and his ministry partners serve as ideal role models in their motivations and work ethic, particularly as we do the work of ministry (vv. 7–9).

2. We work.

> For we hear that there are some among you who are idle. They are not busy but busybodies. Now we command and exhort such people by the Lord Jesus Christ to work quietly and provide for themselves. But as for you, brothers and sisters, do not grow weary in doing good. (2 Thess. 3:11–13)

Paul had clear advice for those who were idle busybodies: work quietly and earn their own living (vv. 11–12) and "do not grow weary in doing good" (v. 13). In a previous letter, he included teachings to live quietly, for people to mind their own business, and to avoid inappropriate dependence on others. This demonstrates godly behavior to a watching world (1 Thess. 4:11–12).

3. We warn.

> If anyone does not obey our instruction in this letter, take note of that person; don't associate with him, so that he may be ashamed. Yet don't consider him as an enemy, but warn him as a brother. (2 Thess. 3:14–15)

God calls us to be generous to those with genuine needs, but we are not obligated to support self-professing Christians who are unwilling to work (2 Thess. 3:10). Instead, we exercise church discipline, pulling away from them and warning them of the consequences of idle living (2 Thess. 3:14–15). Perhaps the embarrassment might lead that person to repent and take personal responsibility (v. 14).

Life with God

Laziness, freeloading, and being a busybody are some of the ways that sin affects our work. But the grace of God is sufficient, both to empower our work and to forgive us when we fall short. Regardless of what we do throughout the day, our motivation as Christians is clear:

> Whatever you do, in word or in deed, do everything in the name of the Lord Jesus, giving thanks to God the Father through him. (Col. 3:17)

For Reflection and Discussion

Use these two pages to respond to the following questions, to record your prayers to God, and/or to prepare to process this information with others.

1. Which role models do you want to imitate in these matters? What, specifically, do you appreciate about them?
2. As you consider the responsibilities God has for you, where are you falling short?
3. What are some practical ways that you could be more faithful to God in these areas?

12. Give Financially

The Bible has much to say both about the way we *view* money and the way we *use* money. For example, we must see the danger in overvaluing money and the consequences of doing so:

- "No one can serve two masters, since either he will hate one and love the other, or he will be devoted to one and despise the other. You cannot serve both God and money." (Matt. 6:24)
- "For the love of money is a root of all kinds of evil, and by craving it, some have wandered away from the faith and pierced themselves with many griefs." (1 Tim. 6:10)

It is necessary, however, to spend money, whether for food, clothing, or shelter. There is also wisdom in storing up some resources for the future. But one of the primary reasons God has entrusted us with money is so that we can give it away, particularly as we contribute financially to our local churches.

God does not need money, for he is the source, owner, and provider of all good things (Ps. 50:10–12). But he commands that we give financially for a variety of reasons (1 Cor. 16:2). As we obey God, he progressively aligns our hearts and minds with his own.

What follows are various lessons from 2 Corinthians 8–9. These chapters contain the most concentrated teaching in the Bible about Christian giving.

First, let's define the *significance* of Christian giving.

1. Christian giving highlights God's grace that comes to us and then flows through us to others.

- "Now as you excel in everything—in faith, speech, knowledge, and in all diligence, and in your love for us—excel also in this act of grace." (2 Cor. 8:7)
- "And God is able to make every grace overflow to you, so that in every way, always having everything you need, you may excel in every good work." (2 Cor. 9:8)

2. Christian giving provides for others in the body of Christ.

At the present time your surplus is available for their need, so that their abundance may in turn meet your need, in order that there may be equality. (2 Cor. 8:14)

3. Christian giving results in thanksgiving to God.

You will be enriched in every way for all generosity, which produces thanksgiving to God through us. (2 Cor. 9:11)

4. Christian giving finds its source and meaning at the cross.

For you know the grace of our Lord Jesus Christ: Though he was rich, for your sake he became poor, so that by his poverty you might become rich. (2 Cor. 8:9)

5. Christian giving results in God receiving the glory.

Because of the proof provided by this ministry, they will glorify God for your obedient confession of the gospel of Christ, and for your generosity in sharing with them and with everyone. (2 Cor. 9:13)

Life with God

As you think about supporting your local church financially, what are the *characteristics* of Christian giving? Christian giving is:

- generous, not stingy (2 Cor. 8:2),
- voluntary, not enforced (2 Cor. 8:3),
- enthusiastic, not grudging (2 Cor. 8:4),
- sensible, not reckless (2 Cor. 8:12), and
- deliberate, not haphazard (2 Cor. 9:7).[30]

In the process of giving away our financial resources and sharing our possessions, several things happen. We express our desire for the advancement of God's work. We cherish our local churches and how God is using them. And, ultimately, we celebrate God as the Giver of all good things, particularly the gift of Jesus (James 1:17; Rom. 5:15).

---

[30] Taken from Harris, *The Second Epistle to the Corinthians*, 124.

For Reflection and Discussion

Use these two pages to respond to the following questions, to record your prayers to God, and/or to prepare to process this information with others.

1. Why should you prioritize giving to your own local church?
2. When considering the *significance* of Christian giving, which of the five points above seem particularly meaningful to you? Why?
3. When considering the *characteristics* of Christian giving, evaluate your own habits of giving. In what ways might God want you to change your habits of giving (particularly to your local church)?

13. Use Your Spiritual Gifts

The apostle Paul calls us to dedicate ourselves holistically to God, in both body and mind:

> Therefore, brothers and sisters, in view of the mercies of God, I urge you to present your bodies as a living sacrifice, holy and pleasing to God; this is your true worship. Do not be conformed to this age, but be transformed by the renewing of your mind, so that you may discern what is the good, pleasing, and perfect will of God. (Rom. 12:1–2)

As an act of worship, we present our bodies to God as living sacrifices (v. 1), as opposed to presenting ourselves "to sin as weapons [or instruments] for unrighteousness" (Rom. 6:13).

And instead of being conformed to this world, we are transformed by the renewing of our minds (Rom. 12:2; see John 17:17; 2 Tim. 3:16–17; Heb. 4:11–13).

Paul then explains how his teaching in verses 1–2 applies as we relate to others within our churches. What truths do we learn about ourselves and life in community?

1. We think about ourselves from God's perspective.

> For by the grace given to me, I tell everyone among you not to think of himself more highly than he should think. Instead, think sensibly, as God has distributed a measure of faith to each one. (Rom. 12:3)

Apart from God's guidance and work in our lives, we distort the truth about ourselves in one of two ways. Either we believe that we have little or no value or we think of ourselves more highly than we ought (v. 3). When we see ourselves from God's perspective, we think about ourselves sensibly, according to "the varying degrees of faith God has given to each believer or the Christian faith that all believers hold in common."[31] In the process, we recognize that God gives the grace and we receive

---

[31] *NIVBTSB*, 2,041.

the grace. There is, therefore, no reason for pride within Christians, for every good gift is from God (James 1:17).

2. We recognize that we are members of the body of Christ.

> Now as we have many parts in one body, and all the parts do not have the same function, in the same way we who are many are one body in Christ and individually members of one another. (Rom. 12:4–5)

The human body consists of different parts, and those parts have different functions (v. 4). In a like manner, the one body of Christ consists of different individuals with different contributions to make, and we are members of one another (v. 5). The apostle Paul expands on this imagery greatly in 1 Corinthians 12. It is natural, then, to ask how each of us can contribute to the larger body of Christ.

3. We use our gifts to benefit others.

> According to the grace given to us, we have different gifts: If prophecy, use it according to the proportion of one's faith; if service, use it in service; if teaching, in teaching; if exhorting, in exhortation; giving, with generosity; leading, with diligence; showing mercy, with cheerfulness. (Rom. 12:6–8)

The answer is that we use our spiritual gifts, which are Spirit-empowered abilities that God gives us for the strengthening of the church. Here, the gifts include prophecy, service, teaching, and other manifestations. For each of us, we exercise the gift in a way that is fitting to the gift and beneficial for others.

Life with God

As for specific spiritual gifts in our lives, we *benefit* from them, *identify* them in ourselves and others, *develop* them, and *use* them for the good of others and the glory of God. This is part of what it means to present our bodies to God (Rom. 12:1). And while the immediate goal of using our spiritual gifts is to serve others, the ultimate goal is "that God may be glorified through Jesus Christ in everything. To him be the glory and the power forever and ever. Amen" (1 Pet. 4:11).

For Reflection and Discussion

Use these two pages to respond to the following questions, to record your prayers to God, and/or to prepare to process this information with others.

1. How do you undervalue or overvalue yourself? For one or both of those tendencies, how has it affected your ability to serve God faithfully?
2. How have you benefited from the spiritual gifts of others?
3. What specific steps might you take to identify, develop, and use your spiritual gifts for the benefit of others and the glory of God?

14. Love Your Neighbor

To love God the Father with all your heart, soul, and mind is Jesus's "greatest and most important command" (Matt. 22:37–38). The second great commandment, Jesus tells us, is to "love your neighbor as yourself" (Matt. 22:39; see Lev. 19:18).

Leviticus 19:9–18 is a central passage in helping us to understand love in concrete terms. For the Israelites, their "neighbors" were primarily those inside their community, those within their direct sphere of influence. How, then, do we love our neighbors?[32]

1. We love others with our possessions.

> "When you reap the harvest of your land, you are not to reap to the very edge of your field or gather the gleanings of your harvest. Do not strip your vineyard bare or gather its fallen grapes. Leave them for the poor and the resident alien; I am the LORD your God." (Lev. 19:9–10)

God required his people in the Old Testament to be generous by making parts of their crops available to the poor. In a like manner, God calls his people in the New Testament to be generous and care for those in need (Acts 4:32–37; 2 Cor. 9:11; Eph. 4:28).

2. We love others with our words.

> "Do not steal. Do not act deceptively or lie to one another. Do not swear falsely by my name, profaning the name of your God; I am the LORD." (Lev. 19:11–12)

One way we express love for others is by speaking according to the truth. We do not lie or swear falsely. We love and speak truth, whether in business, in the courts, in our homes, or in our churches.

3. We love others by our actions.

> "Do not oppress your neighbor or rob him. The wages due a hired worker must not remain with you until morning. Do not

---

[32] I follow DeYoung and Gilbert's outline, *What Is the Mission of the Church?*, 143–147.

curse the deaf or put a stumbling block in front of the blind, but you are to fear your God; I am the LORD." (Lev. 19:13–14)

Love does not take advantage of those who are vulnerable, financially or otherwise. Behaviors like oppression, robbery, and cursing a deaf person are evil. Instead, we fear/revere God himself, and that motivation shapes our behaviors.

4. We love others in our judgments.

"Do not act unjustly when deciding a case. Do not be partial to the poor or give preference to the rich; judge your neighbor fairly. Do not go about spreading slander among your people; do not jeopardize your neighbor's life; I am the LORD." (Lev. 19:15–16)

Inside and outside of courts, we seek justice—judgments that are in accord with the truth, not showing partiality or playing favorites. We protect others by refusing to slander and put them in harm's way.

5. We love others in our attitude.

"Do not harbor hatred against your brother. Rebuke your neighbor directly, and you will not incur guilt because of him. Do not take revenge or bear a grudge against members of your community, but love your neighbor as yourself; I am the LORD." (Lev. 19:17–18)

Love is a matter of our hearts, words, and hands. We do not hate, we reason directly with others, and we do not take vengeance or bear grudges. We love others just as we would love ourselves.

Life with God

Each of these five groupings of verses end with the pronouncement from God "I am the LORD" (vv. 10, 12, 14, 16, 18), for we live in his presence, under his lordship, and according to his laws. While we cannot address every need we see or read about, our "neighbors" are all around us, with needs well within our power to help. The key, Jesus tells us, is to be the neighbor that God want us to be (Luke 10:36).

For Reflection and Discussion

Use these two pages to respond to the following questions, to record your prayers to God, and/or to prepare to process this information with others.

1. For each of the five ways we express love for others, identify and explain how God might be calling you to mature.
2. Why does God repeat himself: "I am the LORD"? What, practically speaking, does it mean to live in light of God's presence and authority?
3. What prevents you from loving others as yourself? What concrete steps can you take to demonstrate love to those closest to you?

15. Care for Creation

As we grow in the Christian faith, our God-given responsibilities become more apparent, whether within our families, at church, or at work. We also have a set of responsibilities to God for creation itself.

These responsibilities raise important questions. What is a basic theology of creation? And how does God want us to care for creation?

1. God created all people and things to display his glory.

- "The heavens declare the glory of God, and the expanse proclaims the work of his hands." (Ps. 19:1)
- "Everyone who bears my name and is created for my glory. I have formed them; indeed, I have made them." (Isa. 43:7)
- "Then God said, 'Let us make man in our image, according to our likeness. They will rule the fish of the sea, the birds of the sky, the livestock, the whole earth, and the creatures that crawl on the earth.'" (Gen. 1:26)

All of creation declares the glory of God (Ps. 19:1). Humans are part of creation, and God created us to glorify him—to see, to experience, and to express his supreme importance and excellence (Isa. 43:7). We are made in his image, which means that we rule on his behalf and serve as steward-managers of his creation (Gen. 1:26).

2. God subjected creation to futility when humanity sinned.

> For the creation was subjected to futility—not willingly, but because of him who subjected it—in the hope that the creation itself will also be set free from the bondage to decay into the glorious freedom of God's children. For we know that the whole creation has been groaning together with labor pains until now. (Rom. 8:20–22)

When Adam and Eve sinned (Gen. 3:6), God brought the judgment he promised (Gen. 2:17; 5:5; Rom. 2:5). Death spread to all humanity (Rom. 5:12), and the rest of creation suffered consequences as well (Gen. 3:17–18), which is described as subjection to futility, bondage to decay, and a time of groaning (Rom. 8:20–22). Therefore, all of creation fell into a corrupted state. And therefore all of creation needs restoration.

3. God makes all things new in and through Jesus Christ.

- "Therefore, if anyone is in Christ, he is a new creation; the old has passed away, and see, the new has come!" (2 Cor. 5:17)
- "The creation itself will also be set free from the bondage to decay into the glorious freedom of God's children." (Rom. 8:21)

When someone turns to Jesus, he or she becomes part of the new creation that God has established in Christ, which includes a new way of thinking and living (2 Cor. 5:14–17).[33] This is a foretaste of when God will completely renew all people and things—in the new heavens and the new earth (Rom. 8:21; Rev. 21:1–5).

Life with God

Douglas and Jonathan Moo outline our main responsibilities to creation by using the acronym "AWAKE":[34]

> We are challenged to be *Attentive* to the community of creation around us, to *Walk* more and consider how and where and how much we travel, to become *Activists* for God's kingdom on earth, speaking up and working on behalf of his creation, to reject our culture's way of *Konsumerism*,[35] and to *Eat* joyfully, thankfully, reverently, and ethically.

These are not the only ways that we live within and care for creation. But, as image bearers of God who steward-manage his creation, we should do no less. Caring for creation is yet one more way that we express our love for God and willingness to obey him.

---

[33] Moo & Moo, *Creation Care*, 139–141.
[34] Ibid., 234.
[35] An intentional misspelling by the authors. See 231–232.

For Reflection and Discussion

Use these two pages to respond to the following questions, to record your prayers to God, and/or to prepare to process this information with others.

1. How has sin affected you personally and the world around you? What evidence do you see of a corrupted creation?
2. How is God making all things new in Christ (2 Cor. 5:17; Rev. 21:5)? Has he done so in your life? If so, what evidence do you see?
3. How can you care for creation more faithfully? How do you, at times, value the creation more than you value the Creator?

Guide for Meeting with Others

Open with Prayer

Recite Memory Verses

For Discussion

1. Give Financially (from Lesson 12)
   a. Review the main points from that lesson.
   b. Why should you prioritize giving to your own local church?
   c. When you consider the *significance* of Christian giving, which of the five points from that lesson seem particularly meaningful to you?
   d. When you consider the *characteristics* of Christian giving, evaluate your own habits of giving. In what ways might God want you to change your habits of giving (particularly to your local church)?

2. Use Your Spiritual Gifts (from Lesson 13)
   a. Read Romans 12:1–2. What are the apostle Paul's main points from verses 1–2? How can you apply these truths in your life?
   b. Read Romans 12:3–5. Why is it tempting to think too highly of ourselves, and what is the remedy or solution? Explain the metaphor that Christians constitute one body. What are the implications for our lives?
   c. Read Romans 12:6–8. How have you benefitted from the spiritual gifts of others? How can you specifically contribute to strengthening your local church?

3. Responding to God
   a. What part of the lessons on the preceding pages did you find to be the most helpful or challenging? Why?
   b. Name one or more of your desires that you want to bring to God in prayer (for yourself and/or for others).

Pray for One Another

Notes

Notes

Unit Four:
We Help Non-Christians to Know God

Overview

Introduction

God calls us to serve others whether they are Christians or not—within our families, in our communities, and at work. But when we discover that someone is not a Christian, perhaps the most profound way to express love is to share how he or she can enter a personal relationship with God through Jesus Christ. If the situation was reversed, isn't that what you would want someone to do for you (to help you know God)?

Christians and non-Christians alike need to learn more about God the Father, reflect on the nature and consequences of their sins, and hear the gospel message that Jesus died and rose from the dead. But the lessons in this unit emphasize taking the message of the gospel to those who do not yet know God through Jesus Christ. You will study passages such as Mark 13:10, Luke 24:44–49, John 20:21, Acts 1:8, and 2 Corinthians 5:18–21. Passages like these will shape your thinking about the church's evangelistic responsibility and how you can contribute.

This unit explores the question, "How can we help non-Christians to know God through Jesus Christ?"

Reading

Read lessons sixteen through twenty.

Memory Verses

- "Therefore, we are ambassadors for Christ, since God is making his appeal through us. We plead on Christ's behalf: 'Be reconciled to God.'" (2 Cor. 5:20)
- "He also said to them, 'This is what is written: The Messiah would suffer and rise from the dead the third day, and repentance for forgiveness of sins would be proclaimed in his name to all the nations, beginning at Jerusalem.'" (Luke 24:46–47)

16. Take the Gospel Message to Others

Some Christians do not remember when they first turned from their sins and trusted in Jesus, perhaps because they committed themselves to him at an early age. But many people do remember the moment when they called on the name of the Lord Jesus for salvation. Whether people remember when they believed or not, the Bible affirms that "everyone who calls on the name of the Lord will be saved" (Rom. 10:13). But how did we come to call on Jesus's name? What steps occurred prior to our conversions?

The apostle Paul explains the progression through a series of rhetorical questions, which I outline in four steps. In brief, one or more people had to carry the message to us that Jesus died and rose from the dead. That is the heart of the gospel. I italicize certain verses below to highlight this progression.

1. In order to call on Jesus for salvation, we had to believe.

> *How, then, can they call on him they have not believed in?* And how can they believe without hearing about him? And how can they hear without a preacher? (Rom. 10:14)

2. In order for us to believe, we had to hear the gospel.

> How, then, can they call on him they have not believed in? *And how can they believe without hearing about him?* And how can they hear without a preacher? (Rom. 10:14)

3. In order for us to hear the gospel, someone had to proclaim it to us.

> How, then, can they call on him they have not believed in? And how can they believe without hearing about him? *And how can they hear without a preacher?* (Rom. 10:14)

4. In order to proclaim the gospel to us, someone had to be sent.

> *And how can they preach unless they are sent?* As it is written: "How beautiful are the feet of those who bring good news." (Rom. 10:15)

To reverse the order: "preachers are sent, the preachers proclaim the message, people hear the message, and those who hear believe."[36]

And how do people respond when they hear the gospel?

> But not all obeyed the gospel. For Isaiah says, "Lord, who has believed our message?" So faith comes from what is heard, and what is heard comes through the message about Christ. (Rom. 10:16–17)

When people hear the good news that Jesus died and rose from the dead, they respond in one of two ways. Some refuse to turn from their sin and trust in Jesus. In that way, they do not respond obediently to the call of the gospel (Rom. 10:16). Others turn from their sin and trust in Jesus, precisely because they heard the word about Jesus Christ (Rom. 10:17).

Life with God

> Jesus said to them again, "Peace to you. As the Father has sent me, I also send you." (John 20:21; see John 20:31)

God the Father sent Jesus to save the world, and yet people must trust in him (John 3:16–17). As God sent Jesus into the world, so Jesus sent the disciples into the world (John 20:21) to witness to Jesus's death and resurrection (Acts 1:8), to proclaim repentance and forgiveness (Luke 24:47), and to make disciples (Matt. 28:19). Collectively, that is the work we are compelled to do.

We contribute to this work when we pray, give financially to churches, and serve. But the gospel is good news that must be proclaimed and explained with our words. We carry the message that Jesus died and rose from the dead to bring people to God the Father. And then we help them to understand the choice they now face.

---

[36] *NIVBTSB*, 2,038.

For Reflection and Discussion

Use these two pages to respond to the following questions, to record your prayers to God, and/or to prepare to process this information with others.

1. In light of Romans 10:13–15, how did you come to call on Jesus's name? For example, who did God send? What did that person say to you? How did you respond?
2. What specifically has Jesus sent us to do?
3. How does your local church advance this mission? How can you participate more actively?

17. Introduce People to God the Father

Before you became a Christian (assuming you have done so), your relationship to God was broken, alienated, and unreconciled. In fact, Paul's words could be applied to every non-Christian:

> They are darkened in their understanding, excluded from the life of God, because of the ignorance that is in them and because of the hardness of their hearts. (Eph. 4:18)

We, too, were "excluded from the life of God" (Eph. 4:18). Elsewhere, we read that we were "enemies" of God (Rom. 5:10) and in a state of "hostility" with him (Eph. 2:16; Col. 1:21). But now, as Christians, we embrace the privilege and responsibility to help others enter a right, reconciled relationship with God. In the following passage I use brackets [ ] to clarify whether God the Father or Jesus is in view. Then, I will clarify the meaning of the passage.

> Everything is from God [the Father], who has reconciled us to himself through Christ and [God the Father] has given us the ministry of reconciliation. That is, in Christ, God [the Father] was reconciling the world to himself, not counting their trespasses against them, and he [God the Father] has committed the message of reconciliation to us. Therefore, we are ambassadors for Christ, since God [the Father] is making his appeal through us. We plead on Christ's behalf: "Be reconciled to God [the Father]." He [God the Father] made the one who did not know sin [Jesus] to be sin for us, so that in him [Jesus] we might become the righteousness of God [the Father]. (2 Cor. 5:18–21)

What is the nature of our ministry before God?[37]

1. The basis of our ministry is our own reconciliation to God.

> Everything is from God, who has reconciled us to himself through Christ and has given us the ministry of reconciliation. That is, in Christ, God was reconciling the world to himself, not counting their

---

[37] I adapted this outline from Scott Hafemann's work in *ESVSB*, 2,230.

trespasses against them, and he has committed the message of reconciliation to us. (2 Cor. 5:18–19)

Before we can introduce others to God through Jesus, we must first be reconciled to God (2 Cor. 5:18). That is where life and joy and peace with God begin (Rom. 5:1, 10–11; 11:15; Col. 1:20).

2. The call of our ministry is on behalf of God and Jesus.

> Therefore, we are ambassadors for Christ, since God is making his appeal through us. We plead on Christ's behalf: "Be reconciled to God." (2 Cor. 5:20)

We are ambassadors for Christ, for he commissions us and we represent him. In doing so, God the Father makes his appeal through us to other people (2 Cor. 5:20).

3. The goal of our ministry is introducing others to God.

> Therefore, we are ambassadors for Christ, since God is making his appeal through us. We plead on Christ's behalf: "Be reconciled to God." (2 Cor. 5:20)

One of Paul's main goals was to call men and women to be reconciled to God (2 Cor. 5:20). His "ministry" and "message" focused on this reconciliation (vv. 18–19).

4. The content of our ministry is Christ's death.

> He made the one who did not know sin to be sin for us, so that in him we might become the righteousness of God. (2 Cor. 5:21)

God the Father credits our sin to Jesus's account and Jesus's righteousness to our account, but only if we trust in Jesus (Rom. 5:1; 2 Cor. 5:21; Phil. 3:9).

Life with God

The non-Christians in your life need many things from you: your love, your prayers, and your acts of service. Ultimately, they need to know how they, too, can be reconciled to God the Father through Jesus. Helping them know how they, too, can know God through Jesus Christ is one of the most loving things we can do. This responsibility is one that we carry with us wherever we go.

For Reflection and Discussion

Use these two pages to respond to the following questions, to record your prayers to God, and/or to prepare to process this information with others.

1. What does it mean if two people are unreconciled? What does it mean if they become reconciled? What, then, does it mean that we have a ministry of reconciliation (between God and others)?
2. What should we tell others about God even before we tell them about Jesus? See, for example, Acts 14:14–17 and 17:22–31.
3. What does it mean to be an ambassador? What obstacles stand in the way of you becoming a more effective ambassador for Jesus Christ? How can you overcome those obstacles?

18. Explain and Confront Sin

Throughout the Bible, God explains and confronts sin in a variety of ways. For example, see Genesis 3, Isaiah 1, Jeremiah 2, and Romans 1:18–3:20.

Every sin we commit has this in common: we displace God from the center of our lives, focusing instead on someone or something else we believe to be more worthy, more attractive, or more satisfying. In countless ways, we deviate from God's will as revealed in the Bible.

Matthew 19:16–22 outlines the way Jesus confronted sin in the life of a rich, young ruler. This passage helps us understand sin, both in our own lives and in the lives of others. As it relates to sharing our faith, however, what principles can we follow?

1. We direct people to God.

> Just then someone came up and asked him, "Teacher, what good must I do to have eternal life?" "Why do you ask me about what is good?" he said to him. "There is only one who is good." (Matt. 19:16–17)

The young man asked Jesus what good (or good deed) he must perform to have eternal life (v. 16). Before addressing the question, Jesus directed his attention to God the Father: "There is only one who is good" (v. 17). Here, Jesus was not denying his own moral goodness. Instead, Jesus established that all questions of religious performance and eternal life must take place under the umbrella of God the Father's character, actions, and expectations, which are perfect. He is the ultimate standard and starting point.

2. We explain God's expectations.

> "If you want to enter into life, keep the commandments." "Which ones?" he asked him. Jesus answered: "Do not murder; do not commit adultery; do not steal; do not bear false witness; honor your father and your mother; and love your neighbor as yourself." (Matt. 19:17–19)

When Jesus said, "Keep the commandments," he was not suggesting that the young man could earn eternal life. Instead, Jesus was likely "setting the man up to realize what he is still missing."[38] In his response, Jesus assumed the reality that God reveals his laws and holds us accountable to those laws.

3. We challenge sin in others.

> "I have kept all these," the young man told him. "What do I still lack?" "If you want to be perfect," Jesus said to him, "go, sell your belongings and give to the poor, and you will have treasure in heaven. Then come, follow me." When the young man heard that, he went away grieving, because he had many possessions. (Matt. 19:20–22)

This young man did not understand how far he fell short in the moral realm. But instead of explaining each of the commandments in more detail, Jesus jumped to the heart of the matter and confronted the young man's idolatry—his possessions. In this way, God was not looking for one good deed, but godly sorrow, repentance, and trust. The young man grieved precisely because he loved his possessions more than God. But Jesus made his choice clear.

Life with God

It is not enough to explain what sin is to others. We must call attention to it and challenge it. This does not require us to be harsh. But, like Jesus, we help others see what stands between them and God the Father, whether it is an obsession with possessions, sexual immorality, or greed. For example, if you are talking to a non-Christian friend about the nature of sin, and if you both know and discuss how he regularly gets drunk, talk to him about that sin in particular. With assertiveness, encourage him to turn away from that sin and other sins (as a conscious decision) and turn to God by faith. Love requires no less.

---

[38] *NIVBTSB*, 1,738.

For Reflection and Discussion

Use these two pages to respond to the following questions, to record your prayers to God, and/or to prepare to process this information with others.

1. Why do people need to understand the character and expectations of God the Father *before* they can understand sin?
2. What is the difference between merely *explaining* sin and its consequences and actually *challenging* sin in others' lives?
3. What prevents you from being more assertive in this area? What is the worst that could happen? What is the best that could happen?

19. Proclaim and Explain the Gospel

The biggest problem we face in this life is our personal sin against God. Not only must we reflect on that reality in our own lives but it is our responsibility to encourage others to do so as well. If the wrath of God is currently being revealed against humanity (Rom. 1:18), and if God's future judgment is coming (Rom. 2:5; Heb. 9:27), is there any solution? Any hope?

The gospel of Jesus Christ is that answer. And there is no other answer that brings human beings to God. But what is the gospel?[39]

1. The gospel is good news.

> It is necessary that the gospel be preached to all nations. (Mark 13:10)

The noun *gospel* means "good news," while the verbal forms mean "to proclaim good news." Jesus's followers experience great suffering in this life (Acts 14:22; 2 Cor. 1:8–9; 2 Tim. 3:12). But before Jesus brings our hardships to an end by fully establishing his kingdom on earth, this good news must be proclaimed to all nations (Mark 13:10).

2. The gospel is God's intervention into the world in Jesus.

> God is my witness, whom I serve with my spirit in telling the good news about his Son. (Rom. 1:9)

In the Old Testament, we read of the good news that God would intervene to save his people, producing both immediate and eternal benefits (Isa. 40:9–11; 52:7–10; 61:1–3).[40] In the New Testament, the word *gospel* can refer generally to God's intervention in the world in Christ (Rom. 1:9; Phil. 1:27).[41] So, in the broad sense of the word, the gospel is a shaft of light from God that cuts through the darkness, and that light is Jesus himself (John 1:9).

---

[39] See Chandler and Wilson, *The Explicit Gospel*; Gilbert, *What Is the Gospel?*; Carson, "What Is the Gospel?—Revisited."
[40] Edwards, *The Gospel according to Mark*, 24–25.
[41] Moo, *The Letter to the Romans*, 41.

3. The gospel is Jesus's death and resurrection.

> For I passed on to you as most important what I also received: that Christ died for our sins according to the Scriptures, that he was buried, that he was raised on the third day according to the Scriptures. (1 Cor. 15:3–4)

The center of God's intervention into the world is Jesus's death and resurrection. Those events are the very center of the shaft of light. Any "gospel" that minimizes or ignores Jesus's death and resurrection is not the gospel (Gal. 1:1–10).

4. The gospel is the power for salvation.

> For I am not ashamed of the gospel, because it is the power of God for salvation to everyone who believes, first to the Jew, and also to the Greek. (Rom. 1:16)

The gospel is not merely a set of historical facts, and the gospel does not merely make it possible for people to know God. It is power from God that accomplishes the salvation of his people (Rom. 1:16). The gospel alone makes peace with God.

5. The gospel calls for a response.

> But not all obeyed the gospel. For Isaiah says, "Lord, who has believed our message?" (Rom. 10:16)

"To obey" the gospel means to receive its saving benefits by turning from our sins and trusting in Jesus (Mark 1:15; Rom. 10:16). Repentance and trust are not the gospel, but they are the necessary and most appropriate responses to the gospel.

Life with God

The gospel is for non-Christians (Rom. 15:20), but it is also for Christians (Rom. 1:15). Why? Because the gospel is both the means by which we initially come to God and also the foundational reality that allows us to stay in relationship to God. We receive it (Gal. 1:9), are strengthened by it (Rom. 16:25), proclaim it (Eph. 6:19), and suffer for it (2 Tim. 1:8). Ultimately, the gospel leads to holistic life change. Because of the gospel, we die to sin and live to God, all by the power of the Holy Spirit (Rom. 6:1–11; 8:10–11; Col. 2:12).

For Reflection and Discussion

Use these two pages to respond to the following questions, to record your prayers to God, and/or to prepare to process this information with others.

1. What is the gospel of Jesus Christ (both in the broad and the narrow senses of the word)?
2. How does the gospel make it possible to come to God?
3. What are some of the most appropriate responses to the gospel? How does the gospel make practical differences in your life?

20. Proclaim Repentance and Forgiveness

The Scriptures clearly affirm that Jesus is alive and how that knowledge should transform our lives. Because he is alive—even now reigning at the right hand of God—then nothing is more important than worshiping Jesus and obeying him.

After God raised Jesus from the dead (Acts 2:24), Jesus appeared to the disciples to convince them of this very fact:

> "Why are you troubled?" he asked them. "And why do doubts arise in your hearts? Look at my hands and my feet, that it is I myself! Touch me and see, because a ghost does not have flesh and bones as you can see I have." (Luke 24:38–39)

Jesus showed them his hands and feet (vv. 39–40), and he ate with them to provide them with additional evidence of his resurrection (vv. 41–43).

What, then, did he explain and commission his disciples to do? And what must we believe and do?

1. We trust the Bible's teaching about Jesus and submit to its authority.

> He told them, "These are my words that I spoke to you while I was still with you—that everything written about me in the Law of Moses, the Prophets, and the Psalms must be fulfilled." Then he opened their minds to understand the Scriptures. He also said to them, "This is what is written: The Messiah would suffer and rise from the dead the third day." (Luke 24:44–46)

Jesus's authority to commission the disciples is grounded in the Scriptures, which are from God himself (2 Tim. 3:16). The Scriptures, including the Law of Moses, the Prophets, and the Psalms (Luke 22:44), pointed to Jesus all along. After opening their minds to understand what was written (v. 45), Jesus explained that the entire Old Testament pointed to his death and resurrection as the highpoint of God's redemptive plan (v. 46).[42] This is the good news of the gospel (1 Cor. 15:1–4). Not only do

---

[42] *NIVBTSB*, 1,885.

we ourselves believe the gospel but we proclaim and explain the gospel to others as the reality that makes forgiveness possible (Eph. 1:7; 1 John 1:9).

2. We call people to turn from their sin and receive forgiveness.

> "Repentance for forgiveness of sins would be proclaimed in his name to all the nations, beginning at Jerusalem." (Luke 24:47)

After we explain to others that Jesus's death and resurrection makes a way to God the Father, we call for repentance—for people to turn from their sin (v. 47). In the process, we simultaneously call for people to trust in Jesus (Acts 20:21). If people turn to God, they receive forgiveness. This is the message Christians proclaim to all the nations (Luke 24:47).

3. We witness in the power of the Holy Spirit.

> "You are witnesses of these things. And look, I am sending you what my Father promised. As for you, stay in the city until you are empowered from on high." (Luke 24:48–49)

Contemporary Christians stand in a long line of people who trust in Jesus—a line that stretches back to the men and women who witnessed Jesus's death and resurrection with their own eyes (v. 48; Acts 3:15). And it is the Holy Spirit who empowers each of us as we take that message to the ends of the earth (Luke 24:49; Acts 1:8).

Life with God

Jesus's commission in Luke 24 is clear. Based on the authority of Scripture and Jesus himself, we proclaim and explain that Jesus died and rose from the dead. Then, we call people to turn from their sin and to receive forgiveness. If they lack knowledge about God the Father (which is true of most people), we begin there (Acts 14:15–17; 17:24–31). And then we explain the nature of sin and its consequences (John 3:36; Rom. 2:5; 3:9–20; 3:23; 6:23). Only then will people understand the choice that stands before them.

For Reflection and Discussion

Use these two pages to respond to the following questions, to record your prayers to God, and/or to prepare to process this information with others.

1. Summarize Luke 24:44–46 in your own words. What does it mean to be a witness *to* Jesus and a witness *for* Jesus?
2. How would you explain the concepts of *repentance* and *forgiveness* to others?
3. What is the role of the Holy Spirit in your witnessing? How can you be more responsive to the Holy Spirit's ministry in this area of your life?

Guide for Meeting with Others

Open with Prayer

Recite Memory Verses

For Discussion

1. The Process of Evangelism (part one)

    a. Read Romans 10:13–17. Explain the apostle Paul's logic from one verse to the next. What might it look like in your life context to "go" to others?
    b. Read 2 Corinthians 5:18–21. Verse by verse, explain the meaning of the passage. As you do so, pay particular attention both to God the Father's work and Jesus's work. Who is doing what?
    c. Read Acts 17:22–34, focusing on verses 24–31 in particular. What did the apostle Paul teach others about God the Father (both his character attributes and his works)? Then, summarize your findings: What do we need to explain to non-Christians about God the Father?

2. The Process of Evangelism (part two)

    a. Read Matthew 19:16–22. Explain Jesus's intention in verse 21. How can we use a similar approach as we talk to others?
    b. Read 1 Corinthians 15:1–4. What is the gospel? How does it establish the path to God?
    c. Read Luke 24:44–49 and Galatians 2:16. Explain the concepts of "repentance" and "trusting in Jesus."

3. Responding to God

    a. What part of the lessons on the preceding pages did you find to be the most helpful or challenging? Why?
    b. Name one or more of your desires that you want to bring to God in prayer (for yourself and/or for others).

Pray for One Another

Notes

Notes

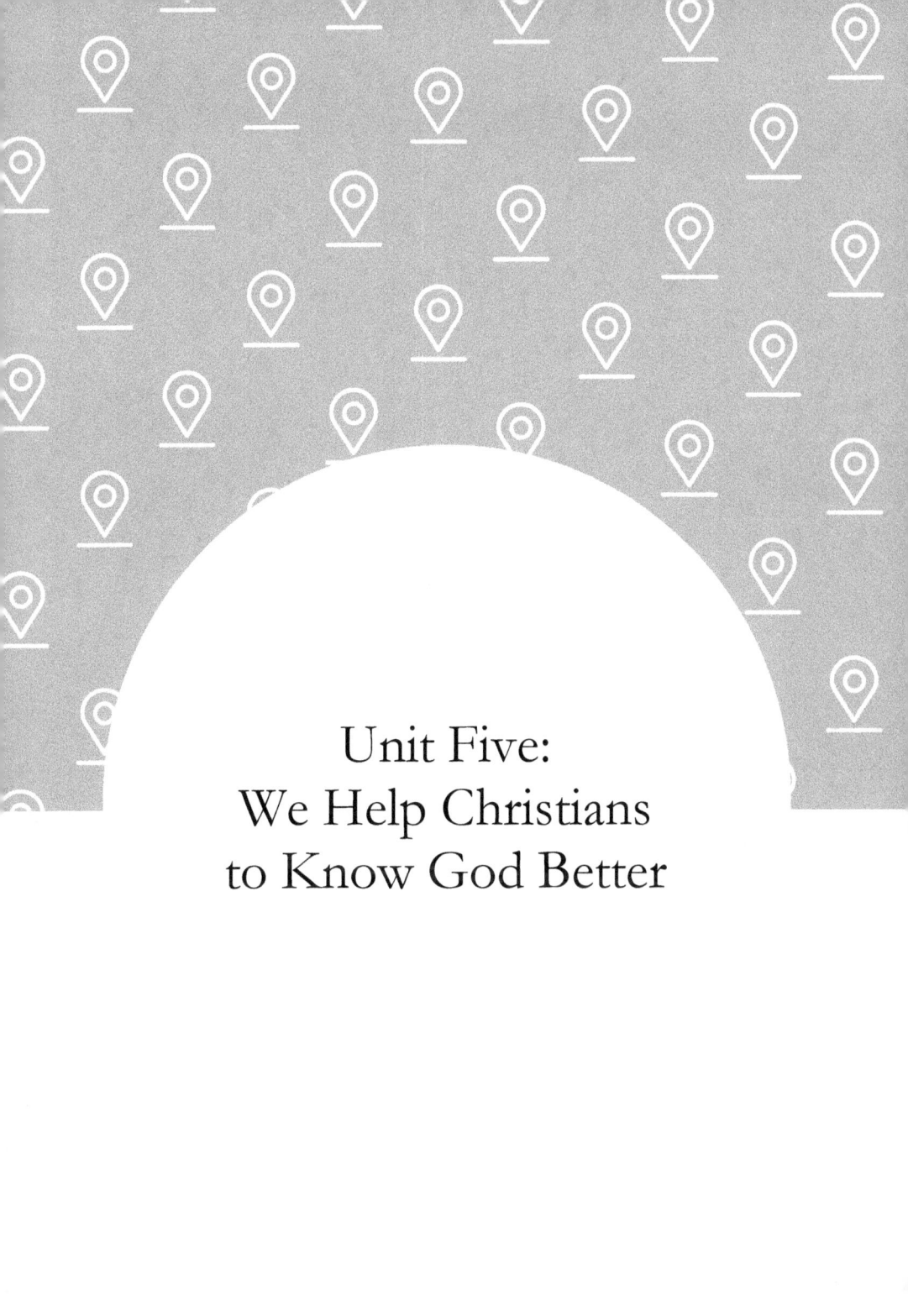

Unit Five:
We Help Christians to Know God Better

Overview

Introduction

When we meet people who are not Christians, one of the most loving things we can do is explain how they can know God through Jesus Christ. That was the focus of the previous unit.

But when we meet people who are Christians, one of the most loving things we can do is to help them to know God better—to encourage them to love and obey Jesus Christ in every area of their lives. The lessons in this unit emphasize how we can encourage fellow Christians accordingly. You will study passages such as Matthew 28:18–20, Mark 8:34–38, 2 Timothy 3:10–4:5, and Titus 2:1–15. Passages like these will shape your thinking about the church's responsibility to help Christians follow Jesus and how you can contribute.

This unit explores the question, "How can we help Christians to know God better?"

Reading

Read lessons twenty-one through twenty-five.

Memory Verses

- "Jesus came near and said to them, 'All authority has been given to me in heaven and on earth. Go, therefore, and make disciples of all nations, baptizing them in the name of the Father and of the Son and of the Holy Spirit, teaching them to observe everything I have commanded you. And remember, I am with you always, to the end of the age.'" (Matthew 28:18–20)
- "Calling the crowd along with his disciples, he said to them, 'If anyone wants to follow after me, let him deny himself, take up his cross, and follow me. For whoever wants to save his life will lose it, but whoever loses his life because of me and the gospel will save it.'" (Mark 8:34–35)

21. Make Disciples

When Christians stand before Jesus at the end of their lives, they need not fear. They have already passed from death to life (John 5:24; 1 John 3:14), and "God's perfect love for believers casts out the fear of wrath and eternal punishment"[43] (1 John 4:18). This does not mean that Christians will avoid Jesus's evaluation:

> For we must all appear before the judgment seat of Christ, so that each may be repaid for what he has done in the body, whether good or evil. (2 Cor. 5:10)

God has given all judgment to Jesus (John 5:22), who will evaluate our work and apportion his rewards (Rev. 22:12).

Whether it is phrased as a question or otherwise, Jesus will address this topic with each of us: "How faithfully did you participate in the task I sent the church to do?"

That task, Matthew 28:19 tells us, is to "make disciples of all nations." This does not mean we have the same gifts or callings from God. But it does mean that making disciples of Jesus Christ is our central task. To be faithful even now, what must we see and do?

1. We submit to Jesus's authority.

> Jesus came near and said to them, "All authority has been given to me in heaven and on earth." (Matt. 28:18)

When the disciples saw the resurrected Jesus in Galilee, some worshiped, and some doubted (Matt. 28:16–17). Jesus began by asserting his authority. "Jesus exercises absolute authority throughout heaven and earth,"[44] precisely because God the Father gave him that authority (Matt. 28:18; 1 Cor. 15:28). Here, Jesus establishes his authority to dictate the mission of the church. Jesus's call "to make disciples of all nations" (Matt. 28:19) is no mere suggestion. It is indeed the Great Commission based on his

---

[43] *ESVSB*, 2,435.
[44] *ESVSB*, 1,888.

right to rule in our lives. Therefore, faithfulness requires that we recognize his authority and submit to it.

2. We make disciples of all nations.

> "Go, therefore, and make disciples of all nations, baptizing them in the name of the Father and of the Son and of the Holy Spirit, teaching them to observe everything I have commanded you." (Matt. 28:19–20)

The main phrase in this passage is Jesus's command for us to "make disciples." This includes both evangelizing non-Christians and discipling Christians to follow Jesus. We make disciples "of all nations" because the scope of our task extends to the end of the earth. This requires that we (1) go to people and to places (as opposed to waiting passively for opportunities), (2) baptize new believers in the one name of the triune God (Father, Son, and Holy Spirit), and (3) teach them to obey all that Jesus commanded (which requires active involvement in their lives).

3. We recognize Jesus's presence with us.

> "And remember, I am with you always, to the end of the age." (Matt. 28:20)

Jesus is "God with us" (Matt. 1:23), the one who is present with his churches to affirm faithfulness and correct unfaithfulness (Matt. 18:20; Rev. 1:12–13, 20; 2–3). His presence guides, empowers, and emboldens us as we seek to make disciples. And this task would be impossible without him.

Life with God

Making disciples of Jesus Christ is the central mission of the church; it is the task he sent us to do. It is our collective mission, in that we strive to accomplish this mission together. And yet each individual Christian must discern how to contribute to that mission in his or her life setting. Though our gifts and callings from God differ, all Christians can pray, give financially, speak of Jesus's death and resurrection, and encourage other Christians using God's Word.

For Reflection and Discussion

Use these two pages to respond to the following questions, to record your prayers to God, and/or to prepare to process this information with others.

1. What makes it difficult, at times, to submit to Jesus's authority?
2. What is the Great Commission? What obstacles stand in the way of you adopting the Great Commission as your own mission in life?
3. What are several ways you can contribute to our great task? How can you grow in your ability to make disciples of Jesus Christ?

22. Explain the Meaning of Following Jesus

A narcotics agent chooses to *follow* a known drug dealer. A reader *follows* a story in a novel. A teenager *follows* a celebrity on social media. But what does it mean to *follow* Jesus Christ? Explaining that concept to others is challenging, precisely because we use this word in a variety of ways.

Jesus said to two fishermen, "Follow me…and I will make you fish for people" (Mark 1:17). On one level, Jesus was calling them to follow after him quite literally, for "immediately they left their nets and followed him" (Mark 1:18). On another level, Jesus had called them to himself—to learn from him, to serve him, and to be in fellowship with others who believe.[45] But this call and their understanding of what it meant would unfold over time.

In Mark 8:34–38, we read some of Jesus's most concentrated teaching on the nature of what it means to follow him and be his disciple. What do we learn about following Jesus?

1. We center our lives on Jesus.

> Calling the crowd along with his disciples, he said to them, "If anyone wants to follow after me, let him deny himself, take up his cross, and follow me." (Mark 8:34)

A *disciple* is a learner or follower of another person and of that person's teachings. Calling a crowd and his disciples to himself, Jesus explained his expectations for those who would follow him. First, a person must deny his or her sinful, self-centered desires (2 Cor. 5:15). Second, a person must take up his or her cross. In the first century, the cross was an instrument of pain and death, the place where someone met his or her end, quite literally. It is an image that declares our death to self and willingness to walk Jesus's path, which might lead to dying as a martyr (Rev. 12:11). Third, a person must follow Jesus as a person, obey his teachings, and do his will (Mark 10:28). These are three of the core expectations of discipleship. And each of them is a call to Christ-centeredness.

---

[45] Edwards, *The Gospel according to Mark*, 48–51.

2. We relinquish our self-centered lives for Jesus's sake.

> "For whoever wants to save his life will lose it, but whoever loses his life because of me and the gospel will save it." (Mark 8:35)

Why should we trust in Jesus and center our lives on him? Among other reasons, preserving (or "saving") one's sinful, self-centered life results in losing life eternally. Denying (or "losing") one's self-centered life for Jesus's sake and the gospel results in eternal life.

3. We recognize the consequences of rejecting Jesus.

> "For what does it benefit someone to gain the whole world and yet lose his life? What can anyone give in exchange for his life?" (Mark 8:36–37)

There is no ultimate benefit when someone forfeits his or her soul for eternity, even if he or she gains the world for a short time. And there is no monetary payment that can be made to secure eternal life.

4. We refuse to be ashamed of Jesus and his words.

> "For whoever is ashamed of me and my words in this adulterous and sinful generation, the Son of Man will also be ashamed of him when he comes in the glory of his Father with the holy angels." (Mark 8:38)

What happens when someone is ultimately embarrassed by Jesus and his words in this life? Jesus will be ashamed and reject that person when he comes in judgment (v. 38). Instead of being ashamed, we boast in Jesus and in him crucified (1 Cor. 1:30–31; Gal. 6:14).

Life with God

In this passage we see our choice: to deny ourselves and follow Jesus or not. Turning from our sins and trusting in Jesus marks the time we become disciples, and yet learning to follow him takes a lifetime. Along the way, we help others to understand Jesus's call on their lives, and so we pass on these truths to the next generation.

For Reflection and Discussion

Use these two pages to respond to the following questions, to record your prayers to God, and/or to prepare to process this information with others.

1. What are the characteristics of someone who follows Jesus?
2. In what ways is your life more self-centered than Christ-centered? What would it look like for you to follow him more attentively and proactively?
3. In what ways are you tempted to be ashamed of Jesus? What would it look like if you were bolder for Jesus in your words and actions?

23. Direct Others to God's Word

As the apostle Paul approached the end of his life, he wrote a final set of instructions to his disciple, Pastor Timothy. While most Christians will never have a formalized preaching ministry like Timothy's (2 Tim. 4:2), each of us will benefit as we study how Paul mentored him. In particular, Paul directed Timothy's attention, again and again, to the centrality of God's Word for all of life and ministry. How do we encourage others to do the same?

1. We encourage others to submit to God's Word.

> But you have followed my teaching, conduct, purpose, faith, patience, love, and endurance, along with the persecutions and sufferings that came to me in Antioch, Iconium, and Lystra. What persecutions I endured—and yet the Lord rescued me from them all. In fact, all who want to live a godly life in Christ Jesus will be persecuted. Evil people and impostors will become worse, deceiving and being deceived. But as for you, continue in what you have learned and firmly believed. You know those who taught you, and you know that from infancy you have known the sacred Scriptures, which are able to give you wisdom for salvation through faith in Christ Jesus. (2 Tim. 3:10–15)

In contrast to false teachers (2 Tim. 3:6–9, 13),[46] Paul called Timothy to follow his example in character and conduct, particularly in persecution and suffering (vv. 10–11). "In fact, all who want to live a godly life in Christ Jesus will be persecuted" (v. 12), while "evil people and impostors" will continue to decay morally (v. 13). In contrast, Timothy had followed Paul's teaching and way of life (v. 10), and Paul wanted him to continue in what he had learned and believed (v. 14). All of this teaching is ultimately based in Scripture itself, which was able to give Timothy "wisdom for salvation through faith in Christ Jesus" (v. 15).

2. We encourage others to see the usefulness of God's Word.

> All Scripture is inspired by God and is profitable for teaching, for rebuking, for correcting, for training in righteousness, so

---

[46] Köstenberger, *Commentary on 1–2 Timothy and Titus*, 34–35.

> that the man of God may be complete, equipped for every good work. (2 Tim. 3:16–17)

As the basis of Paul's charge to Timothy, Paul taught that Scripture is inspired by God and profitable, whether for teaching, correction, or otherwise (v. 16). And this ministry of the Word produces Christians who are complete (or mature) and "equipped for every good work" (v. 17). And those are goals for all of God's people.

3. We encourage others to minister using God's Word.

> I solemnly charge you before God and Christ Jesus, who is going to judge the living and the dead, and because of his appearing and his kingdom: Preach the word; be ready in season and out of season; rebuke, correct, and encourage with great patience and teaching. For the time will come when people will not tolerate sound doctrine, but according to their own desires, will multiply teachers for themselves because they have an itch to hear what they want to hear. They will turn away from hearing the truth and will turn aside to myths. But as for you, exercise self-control in everything, endure hardship, do the work of an evangelist, fulfill your ministry. (2 Tim. 4:1–5)

Paul set the context for his final exhortation: Timothy stood in the presence of God and Jesus Christ, who will judge (or assess) all people (v. 1). At the core of Timothy's ministry was for him to preach/proclaim/herald God's Word, always with a view toward applying God's Word (v. 2). Paul then warned Timothy that people would resist God and the truth of his Word (vv. 3–4), which meant that Timothy had to resolve to fulfill his ministry all the more (v. 5).

Life with God

Observing the way Paul finished his own life inspires all of us to do the same (2 Tim. 4:6–8). He said, "I have fought the good fight, I have finished the race, I have kept the faith" (2 Tim. 4:7). In his life and ours, Word-centeredness is what carries us along until we cross the finish line. Word-centeredness is also what we pass along to others, so they, too, will finish the race.

For Reflection and Discussion

Use these two pages to respond to the following questions, to record your prayers to God, and/or to prepare to process this information with others.

1. To what extent are you submissive to the Word of God? Identify one or more action steps for you to grow in this area.
2. Why must your ministry to others be grounded in God's Word?
3. How can you encourage others to be more Word-centered?

24. Teach Others to Pray

In Matthew 6:9–13, Jesus outlines how we should pray and, therefore, how we should teach others to pray. He said, "Therefore, you should pray like this: Our Father in heaven" (Matt. 6:9; see Luke 11:2–4).

God is the Father of his Son, Jesus Christ (Matt. 11:27; John 1:18), but also the Father to all who believe (John 1:12; Rom. 8:14–17). As we pray, we begin by acknowledging God as Father, the one who guides, provides, and disciplines us for our well-being. He is the one who dwells transcendently "in heaven," ready and willing to fulfill our requests (Matt. 7:7–11). As we pray, and as we teach others to pray, what requests do we make?[47]

1. We pray for God to cause others to honor his name.

"Your name be honored as holy." (Matt. 6:9)

God's name is synonymous with his very being and character. To pray that God's name would be honored as holy is to pray that God would be treated as holy in our thoughts, words, and deeds.

2. We pray for God's kingdom to come.

"Your kingdom come." (Matt. 6:10)

God is the King over all (Isa. 43:15; 1 Tim. 1:17), who has delegated his sovereign rule to Jesus (Ps. 2:6; 1 Cor. 15:28). To pray that God's kingdom would come is to request that God would manifest his rule and reign to a greater extent, even as we long for the fullness of God's kingdom in the future.[48]

3. We pray for God's will to be done.

"Your will be done on earth as it is in heaven." (Matt. 6:10)

A major gap exists between how God's revealed will is perfectly obeyed in heaven and how it is resisted, or achieved incompletely, on earth. This prayer cries out to God that he would bring to pass

---

[47] See Osborne, *Matthew*, 222–234 and Carson, *Matthew*, 200–208.
[48] Osborne, *Matthew*, 228.

his revealed will in the lives of those on earth, both now and at the end of the age.

4. We pray for God to supply our daily needs.

> "Give us today our daily bread." (Matt. 6:11)

This request acknowledges God as the ultimate provider and asks that God would supply each day's need. Here, the request is for food, but God meets all our daily needs (Matt. 6:11, 25–34).

5. We pray for God to forgive our sins.

> "And forgive us our debts, as we also have forgiven our debtors." (Matt. 6:12)

Each sin we commit creates a debt to God, which was paid through Jesus's death (Col. 2:13–14). We ask God to forgive our debts, but when we grasp the depth of our sin and the forgiveness God offers, we are all the more willing to offer forgiveness to others.

6. We pray for God to grant strength and deliverance.

> "And do not bring us into temptation [or testing], but deliver us from the evil one." (Matt. 6:13)

God does not tempt anyone to sin (James 1:13), but he does test (or assess) our faith. Therefore, we ask that God would give us strength in the midst of our temptations or, more likely, spare us from severe trials when our faith is tested.[49] We also pray that he would deliver us from the efforts of Satan, the Evil One.

Life with God

Jesus explicitly instructed his disciples about prayer and modeled prayer for them (Matt. 6:5–15; John 11:41–42; 17:1–26). We learn and teach others to pray by studying Scripture's teachings and by praying together. Over time, the desires of our hearts align more and more with God's revealed will in Scripture (John 14:13). In that way, prayer is not only the means by which we talk to God but it is also one of the ways God transforms our character.

---

[49] Carson, *Matthew*, 207–208.

For Reflection and Discussion

Use these two pages to respond to the following questions, to record your prayers to God, and/or to prepare to process this information with others.

1. What desires do you want to bring to God?
2. In what ways do you want your prayer life to change?
3. What advice would you give to others who are learning how to pray for the first time?

25. Teach the Truth

Teaching one another to obey Jesus Christ is central to the Great Commission. He said, "Go, therefore, and make disciples of all nations...*teaching* them to observe everything I have commanded you" (Matt. 28:19–20, emphasis mine).

By God's grace, we look to all of God's Word to determine what we teach, for "all Scripture is inspired by God and is profitable for teaching, for rebuking, for correcting, for training in righteousness" (2 Tim. 3:16; see 2 Pet. 1:19–21; 3:15–16).

Titus 2:1–15 goes a long way toward helping us understand our task. How do we teach one another to obey?

1. We teach according to one another's age and stage.

- "But you are to proclaim things consistent with sound teaching.
- Older men are to be self-controlled, worthy of respect, sensible, and sound in faith, love, and endurance.
- In the same way, older women are to be reverent in behavior, not slanderers, not slaves to excessive drinking. They are to teach what is good, so that they may encourage the young women to love their husbands and to love their children, to be self-controlled, pure, workers at home, kind, and in submission to their husbands, so that God's word will not be slandered.
- In the same way, encourage the young men to be self-controlled in everything.
- Make yourself an example of good works with integrity and dignity in your teaching. Your message is to be sound beyond reproach, so that any opponent will be ashamed, because he doesn't have anything bad to say about us.
- Slaves are to submit to their masters in everything, and to be well-pleasing, not talking back or stealing, but demonstrating utter faithfulness, so that they may adorn the teaching of God our Savior in everything." (Titus 2:1–10)

The apostle Paul instructed Pastor Titus to "proclaim things consistent with sound teaching" (v. 1). This command includes specific instructions to specific audiences (vv. 2–10). Each of these instructions deserves careful study, reflection, and discussion with other Christians, whether they are directed to older men (v. 2), older and younger women (vv. 3–5), or otherwise. Teaching other Christians to obey is one of the ways we express love (2 John 1–2).

2. We teach according to God's truth.

> For the grace of God has appeared, bringing salvation for all people, instructing us to deny godlessness and worldly lusts and to live in a sensible, righteous, and godly way in the present age, while we wait for the blessed hope, the appearing of the glory of our great God and Savior, Jesus Christ. He gave himself for us to redeem us from all lawlessness and to cleanse for himself a people for his own possession, eager to do good works. Proclaim these things; encourage and rebuke with all authority. Let no one disregard you. (Titus 2:11–15)

Here Paul outlines some of the most foundational truths of the Christian faith (vv. 11–15). God's grace appeared in Jesus Christ, which makes salvation available for all who trust in him (v. 11). God's grace also trains us to renounce sin and to live godly lives (v. 12). We do so as we await the return of Jesus Christ, who is both God and Savior (v. 13). His death redeems people from their sinful ways and claims them as his own possession (v. 14). We must pass on these truths to others. And so we proclaim and explain these truths from the Bible, with authority that is from God himself (v. 15).

Life with God

To follow Jesus, we center ourselves on him and his will for our lives. Doing so requires that we know, teach, and apply the truth of God's Word. In the process, we teach specific people with specific needs. As we keep these truths in mind, God sets us in motion to make followers of Jesus Christ—by building individuals, families, and local churches that honor God. We do so one person at a time.

For Reflection and Discussion

Use these two pages to respond to the following questions, to record your prayers to God, and/or to prepare to process this information with others.

1. To which Christians can you turn for help as you seek to mature in your faith? What, if anything, prevents you from asking for help?
2. Which Christians would benefit from your help? What prevents you from being more proactive in helping others to mature?
3. What strategies can you use to spend more time with those people? To talk more openly? To focus more on God's Word? To pray more regularly?

Guide for Meeting with Others

Open with Prayer

Recite Memory Verses

For Discussion

1. Discipleship

   a. Read Matthew 28:18–20. Explain each part of the passage in detail. What are several ways you can contribute to our great task of making disciples?
   b. Read Mark 8:34–38. Summarize each part of the passage. In what ways is your life more self-centered than Christ-centered? In what ways are you tempted to be ashamed of Jesus?

2. The Word of God and Prayer

   a. Read 2 Timothy 3:10–4:5. What are the main points of the passage? To what extent is your life centered on God's Word? How can you encourage others to be more Word-centered?
   b. Read Matthew 6:9–15. Locate and then explain each of Jesus's six requests of God. For example, the first is "[may] your name be honored as holy" (v. 9). Then, evaluate your own prayer life in light of how Jesus instructs us to pray.

3. Responding to God

   a. What part of the lessons on the preceding pages did you find to be the most helpful or challenging? Why?
   b. Name one or more of your desires that you want to bring to God in prayer (for yourself and/or for others).

Pray for One Another

Notes

Notes

Unit Six:
We Center Our Lives on God (Part I)

Overview

Introduction

To this point in the book, we have explored what it means to embrace our new identity in Christ, pursue Christlike character, serve others, and make disciples as our central mission in life.

But the *ultimate goal* of our lives is not any of these. For example, the ultimate goal of the Christian life is not to embrace the truth that we have been adopted into God's family (assuming we are Christians), and it is not that we help other people when they are in need. Why not? Because God's gifts and doing God's work are not more important than God himself.

Instead, the ultimate, unifying goal of the Christian life is to be God-centered in all that we do. In this unit, I outline five ways that we do so. Because he is the one true God and in accordance with Scripture, we are to:

- listen to God more willingly, attentively, and reverently than to anyone else.
- pray to God as the one who fulfills his precious promises.
- trust in God for salvation and in every other part of our lives.
- hope in God as the one who guarantees the future.
- love God above all else and with every part of our being.

This unit explores the question, "How do we experience and express God-centeredness in our lives?"

Reading

Read lessons twenty-six through thirty.

Memory Verses

> He [Jesus] said to him, "Love the Lord your God with all your heart, with all your soul, and with all your mind. This is the greatest and most important command." (Matt. 22:37–38)

26. Listen to God

God is a talking God. He spoke the universe into existence (Heb. 11:3), and he speaks and reveals himself through nature (Rom. 1:19–20). As it relates to his supernatural revelation, however, God speaks to us through a consistent process. Communication comes from God the Father, through Jesus Christ, through the Holy Spirit, through the written Word, through God's people (who explain God's truth), and finally to us.

When we listen to God through his Word, we are not merely attending to sounds, like listening to chirping birds or falling acorns in a forest. Instead, we focus our attention, seek the meaning of God's words, and apply what we have heard. How and to whom do we listen?

1. We listen to God the Father.

> Long ago God spoke to the fathers by the prophets at different times and in different ways. In these last days, he has spoken to us by his Son. (Heb. 1:1–2)

God speaks in many ways, but he speaks most clearly and profoundly in and through the person of Jesus Christ (John 8:28; Heb. 1:2; Rev. 1:1). God speaks so perfectly in Jesus that Jesus is called the Word of God, the self-expression of God himself (John 1:1, 14).

2. We listen to Jesus Christ.

> Then a voice came from the cloud, saying: "This is my Son, the Chosen One; listen to him!" (Luke 9:35)

God calls us to listen to Jesus (Luke 9:35), for Jesus perfectly reveals the Father and his will for our lives (Matt. 11:27; John 1:18). Jesus is the truth (John 14:6), and he speaks the truth from God (John 8:40), so of course we should listen.

3. We listen to the Holy Spirit.

> "Let anyone who has ears to hear listen to what the Spirit says to the churches." (Rev. 2:7)

In the book of Revelation and elsewhere, God reveals truth to Jesus (Rev. 1:1), who then speaks God's words (Rev. 2:1). As Jesus speaks, the Holy Spirit speaks Jesus's words to us (Rev. 2:7). The Holy Spirit, for example, tells us that we should not harden our hearts (Heb. 3:7–8), particularly as we fight against unbelief (Heb. 3:12).

4. We listen to the triune God through the Bible.

- "All Scripture is inspired by God." (2 Tim. 3:16)
- "Because no prophecy ever came by the will of man; instead, men spoke from God as they were carried along by the Holy Spirit." (2 Pet. 1:21)

The Bible reveals God's will for our lives. It is breathed out or inspired by God (2 Tim. 3:16); records the will, works, and words of Jesus (John 12:49); and reflects the guidance of the Holy Spirit (2 Pet. 1:21). To listen to the words of the Bible is to listen to the triune God.

5. We listen to the triune God through God's people.

- "He himself gave some to be apostles, some prophets, some evangelists, some pastors and teachers." (Eph. 4:11)
- "When you received the word of God that you heard from us, you welcomed it not as a human message, but as it truly is, the word of God, which also works effectively in you who believe." (1 Thess. 2:13)

God speaks both to and through his people, whether they are the first-century apostles, modern-day pastors, or anyone who faithfully helps us understand and obey the Word of God (Rom. 15:4; Eph. 4:11; 1 Thess. 2:13; 4:18; 2 Tim. 4:2).

Life with God

This is a seamless process, beginning in the mind of God and coming to us through God's Word—proclaimed, explained, and applied—so that we encounter God. So when we are Word-centered in Christian community, we are God-centered.

For Reflection and Discussion

Use these two pages to respond to the following questions, to record your prayers to God, and/or to prepare to process this information with others.

1. Summarize the five-fold process in this lesson.
2. What does it mean to be "Word-centered" in practice?
3. What prevents you from being more Word-centered? How can you overcome those obstacles with God's help?

27. Pray to God

My parents told me late one evening that our dog was dying. I was nine years old, perhaps ten. In tears, I ran to the back of the house, kneeled in front of our dusty, lime-green couch, and cried out for God to heal Pretzel. When I woke up the next day, my parents told me that our dog had died. From that time until I was in college, I have no memories of praying to God. I became convinced that prayer was ineffective and I would have to turn elsewhere for help. Why did I come to that conclusion? Put simply, my knowledge of the Bible, and therefore my knowledge of God, was shallow, distorted, and self-centered.

In the Bible, prayer is the way we address God in response to his gracious revelation, whether in worship and thanksgiving or in crying out for help.[50] What do we know about God that makes prayer possible?

- God exists and has always existed (Gen. 1:1; Ps. 90:2).
- God speaks (Gen. 1:3; 2 Tim. 3:16–17).
- God listens (Deut. 26:7; Ps. 66:19).
- God is worthy of praise (1 Tim. 1:17; Rev. 4:11).
- God is faithful to his promises (1 Cor. 10:13; 1 John 1:9).

For these reasons and more, we cry out to God. What do we know about how to express ourselves in prayer?

1. We pray to God the Father.

- "Therefore, you should pray like this: Our Father in heaven, your name be honored as holy." (Matt. 6:9)
- "I always thank my God for you because of the grace of God given to you in Christ Jesus." (1 Cor. 1:4)

While there are examples in the Bible of people praying to Jesus, God the Father is the primary focus. Jesus himself prayed to the Father (Luke 22:42). So Jesus directed the disciples accordingly, not least of which because God's name should be treated as holy

---

[50] Millar, *Calling on the Name of the Lord*.

(Matt. 6:9). The apostle Paul's prayers were God-centered as well, for example, as he thanked God for his grace through Jesus (1 Cor. 1:4).

2. We pray both to and through Jesus Christ.

- "While they were stoning Stephen, he called out: 'Lord Jesus, receive my spirit!'" (Acts 7:59)
- "For through him we both have access in one spirit to the Father." (Eph. 2:18)

Christians should indeed pray to Jesus, just like Stephen in his final moments of life (Acts 7:59–60) or like those who cry out for Jesus to return (1 Cor. 16:22; Rev. 22:20). But the focal point of the New Testament is how Jesus provides access to God, so we can draw near to God and receive forgiveness through Jesus's death (Eph. 2:18; Heb. 7:25; 10:19–22). We pray in Jesus's name to align ourselves with his will, which brings us great joy (John 16:23–24).

3. We pray by the Holy Spirit.

> But you, dear friends, as you build yourselves up in your most holy faith, praying in the Holy Spirit. (Jude 20)

While there are no explicit examples in the Bible of praying to the Holy Spirit, he makes prayer possible. For example, he convicts us of sin (John 16:8) and guides us as we pray (Eph. 6:18; Jude 20). He also prays for us when we do not know how to pray (Rom. 8:26–27).

Life with God

God is listening, Jesus makes a way, and the Holy Spirit guides us, so of course we will pray. We cry out to God in prayer for forgiveness (1 John 1:9), for wisdom (James 1:5), and for others' salvation (Rom. 10:1)—and we thank God in all circumstances (1 Thess. 5:18). These are just some of the ways we pray. In every instance, we communicate to God that he is faithful to keep his promises and that we will trust him. In doing so, prayer aligns us to the will of God.

For Reflection and Discussion

Use these two pages to respond to the following questions, to record your prayers to God, and/or to prepare to process this information with others.

1. In your own words, what is prayer?
2. What interferes with your prayer life before God? What practical steps can you take to overcome those challenges?
3. What do your desires tell you about your own value system? How can you align your heart to God's heart to a greater extent?

28. Trust in God

What makes someone worthy of your trust? First, the person is *willing* to follow through on his or her promises. Second, the person is *able* to follow through on his or her promises. But each of us, at times, falls short in one or both of these areas.

Not so with God. His love toward his people is perfect, and his power is unlimited:

- "Because of the LORD's faithful love we do not perish, for his mercies never end. They are new every morning; great is your faithfulness!" (Lam. 3:22–23)
- "Our God is in heaven and does whatever he pleases." (Ps. 115:3)

God is willing and able to follow through on his promises. Therefore, he is worthy of our trust (Ps. 13:5; 2 Thess. 3:3; Heb. 11:11). When we trust God, we express confidence in him as a person, in his attributes, in his promises, and in his actions, particularly his saving work through Jesus. How do we express trust?

1. We trust in God the Father.

- "But to the one who does not work, but believes on him who declares the ungodly to be righteous, his faith is credited for righteousness." (Rom. 4:5)
- "If we confess our sins, he is faithful and righteous to forgive us our sins and to cleanse us from all unrighteousness." (1 John 1:9)

God is faithful—in his very character and in all he does—and therefore we trust him. His faithfulness expresses itself in a variety of ways. God is faithful to his promises to declare us righteous (Rom. 4:5, 23–25), to forgive us (1 John 1:9), to sanctify/purify us (1 Thess. 5:23–24), and to help us persevere to the end of our lives (1 Cor. 1:8–9). These are some of the ways we trust him to do what he promises to do (John 5:24; 1 Thess. 5:24).

2. We trust in Jesus Christ.

- "And yet because we know that a person is not justified by the works of the law but by faith in Jesus Christ, even we ourselves have believed in Christ Jesus. This was so that we might be justified by faith in Christ." (Gal. 2:16)
- "If we are faithless, he remains faithful, for he cannot deny himself." (2 Tim. 2:13)

God will not declare anyone righteous by his or her own works, but only by trusting in Jesus Christ (Gal. 2:16). Why? Because only his death and resurrection can bring us to God (Rom. 4:25; 1 Pet. 3:18). And once we first trust in Jesus, we continue to trust in him, for he is faithful (2 Tim. 2:11–13), and all the promises of God find their fulfillment and final affirmation in him (2 Cor. 1:19–20).

3. We trust by the Holy Spirit.

- "The purpose was that the blessing of Abraham would come to the Gentiles by Christ Jesus, so that we could receive the promised Spirit through faith." (Gal. 3:14)
- "For we eagerly await through the Spirit, by faith, the hope of righteousness." (Gal. 5:5)

From one perspective, faith is a unique spiritual gift (1 Cor. 12:9). But the Spirit of God works to foster faith in all Christians, precisely as he guides us toward Jesus (John 15:26; 16:13; Gal. 3:14; 5:5).

Life with God

Along with repentance, trust is the means by which we enter a relationship with God (Eph. 2:8–9). By faith, we fight for godly character and battle against sins such as anxiety (Matt. 6:25, 30), pride (Jer. 9:23), and lust (Matt. 5:27–30).[51] By faith we serve God in concrete acts of obedience (Heb. 11). And by faith, we endure suffering and resist temptation until the end of our lives (Rev. 14:12).

---

[51] John Piper's *Battling Unbelief* is worth reading and rereading.

For Reflection and Discussion

Use these two pages to respond to the following questions, to record your prayers to God, and/or to prepare to process this information with others.

1. Do you struggle to trust other people? Why or why not?
2. What makes God the Father and Jesus worthy of your trust? In other words, what makes them so reliable in your life?
3. In what areas of your life do you need to trust God more fully? How would doing so translate into changed behavior?

29. Hope in God

As we age, our limitations become more and more apparent: our strength, stamina, and memory deteriorate over time. Despite our good intentions, our bodies will fail. The trajectory is obvious.

But God is eternal, and he has no such limitations. His knowledge of the future, his ability to bring his will into reality, and his love toward his people are all perfect:

- "Remember what happened long ago, for I am God, and there is no other; I am God, and no one is like me. I declare the end from the beginning, and from long ago what is not yet done, saying: my plan will take place, and I will do all my will." (Isa. 46:9–10)
- "'Though the mountains move and the hills shake, my love will not be removed from you and my covenant of peace will not be shaken,' says your compassionate LORD." (Isa. 54:10)

For these reasons and more, God is a worthy object of our hope, which is a future-oriented faith in the reality that God will fulfill all his promises. How do we express our hope?

1. We hope in God the Father.

- "A king is not saved by a large army; a warrior will not be rescued by great strength. The horse is a false hope for safety; it provides no escape by its great power." (Ps. 33:16–17)
- "Let us hold on to the confession of our hope without wavering, since he who promised is faithful." (Heb. 10:23)
- "Through him you believe in God, who raised him from the dead and gave him glory, so that your faith and hope are in God." (1 Pet. 1:21)

It is tempting to put our hope in people and things other than God, whether it is the way we look, our bank accounts, or our country's military resources (Ps. 33:16–17). How foolish it is, for example, to stare endlessly into the mirror in search of hope. Or how foolish it is to hope in a job to guarantee our future. But

God calls us to direct our hope ultimately to himself. We hope in God because he is faithful to bring all his promises to pass (Heb. 10:23). And our future is certain because God has saved us through Jesus, whom God raised from the dead and glorified for all to see (1 Pet. 1:21).

2. We hope in Jesus Christ.

- "If indeed you remain grounded and steadfast in the faith and are not shifted away from the hope of the gospel that you heard. This gospel has been proclaimed in all creation under heaven, and I, Paul, have become a servant of it." (Col. 1:23)
- "Paul, an apostle of Christ Jesus by the command of God our Savior and of Christ Jesus our hope." (1 Tim. 1:1)

Without Jesus, we have no hope (Eph. 2:12). But Jesus's death and resurrection (Col. 1:23) and his glorious return (Tit. 2:13) anchor our hope. All God's promises find their ultimate fulfillment in Jesus Christ (2 Cor. 1:20), so it is no wonder that Jesus himself is described as "our hope" (1 Tim. 1:1).

3. We hope by the Holy Spirit.

Now may the God of hope fill you with all joy and peace as you believe so that you may overflow with hope by the power of the Holy Spirit. (Rom. 15:13)

It requires a supernatural movement of the Holy Spirit for us to "overflow with [or abound in] hope" (Rom. 15:13)—to see God the Father and God the Son as the objects of our hope.

Life with God

Hoping in God transforms our lives in concrete ways. For example, we seek personal holiness in anticipation of our future transformation (1 John 3:2–3), and we trust in Jesus and grow in our love for people as a result (Col. 1:3–5). We must search the Bible diligently "so that we may have hope through endurance and through the encouragement from the Scriptures" (Rom. 15:4).

For Reflection and Discussion

Use these two pages to respond to the following questions, to record your prayers to God, and/or to prepare to process this information with others.

1. What makes God worthy of your hope?
2. In what ways are you tempted to hope in people and things other than God? Why do you do so? What are the results?
3. How does hope make a practical difference in the way you relate to your family members, your local church, and your community? How does hoping in God affect your decision making?

30. Love God

Love is one of the most flexible words in the English language. A man *loves* to shop at his local grocery store. A woman *loves* her child. And a teenage boy *loves* Chrissy Chrysanthemum—but he lacks the confidence to talk to her.

Words certainly mean different things in different contexts, but what does the Bible have to say about love?

There is a beautiful progression in Scripture regarding love:[52]

- God is love. His devoted affection is part of his very being (1 John 4:8) and focuses eternally on Jesus (John 17:24).
- Love is from God. It is seen in how he meets humanity's physical needs (Matt. 5:45; Acts 14:17), outlines his will for our lives (Ps. 119:124–125; Jude 20–21), and sends Jesus to die for our sins (John 3:16; Rom. 5:8).
- Some people internalize God's love. They realize God's love and receive the benefits (Num. 14:19; Gal. 2:20; Rom. 5:5).
- God's people love God and love others. This is a response to his multifaceted love (Matt. 22:37–40; 1 John 4:7–12, 19).

God's love for his people stretches back before the foundation of the world (Eph. 1:4–5), and his love is everlasting (Rom. 8:31–39). How, then, do we experience and express our love for the triune God?

1. We love God the Father.

- "[Jesus] said to him, 'Love the Lord your God with all your heart, with all your soul, and with all your mind.'" (Matt. 22:37)
- "This is how we know that we love God's children: when we love God and obey his commands. For this is what love for God is: to keep his commands. And his commands are not a burden." (1 John 5:2–3)

---

[52] Two works significantly shaped my thinking here: Carson, *The Difficult Doctrine of the Love of God* and Morgan, "How Does the Trinity's Love Shape Our Love for One Another?"

Jesus brings the heart of God's will into focus, which is to love God the Father with every part of our being (Matt. 22:37–38; Deut. 6:1–9). We do so by directing our ultimate commitment and affection to him, expressed most concretely in our obedience to him (1 John 5:2–3).

2. We love Jesus Christ.

> "The one who has my commands and keeps them is the one who loves me. And the one who loves me will be loved by my Father. I also will love him and will reveal myself to him." (John 14:21)

Loving God the Father is the greatest commandment (Matt. 22:37–38), but it is no less true that we love Jesus. We express our love for Jesus primarily through our obedience to him (John 14:21; 15:9–10). All who love Jesus will be loved by God, be loved by Jesus, and receive more revelation.

3. We love by the Holy Spirit.

> This hope will not disappoint us, because God's love has been poured out in our hearts through the Holy Spirit who was given to us. (Rom. 5:5)

While the Holy Spirit is certainly worthy of our love, one of his primary ministries is to cultivate our love for God the Father, for Jesus, and for others. He not only fills our hearts with love (Rom. 5:5) but he also cultivates our expression of love (Gal. 5:22), such as when we cry out to God in prayer (Gal. 4:6).

Life with God

When we love the things of this world more than God, we express hostility toward him and make ourselves his enemy (James 4:4; 1 John 2:15–17). But if we receive God, our souls become a vase filled with love from God, filled to overflowing (Rom. 5:5). In addition to loving God, we love our neighbors as ourselves (Matt. 22:39). In the process, we express a particular devotion for those in the family of faith (Matt. 25:40; 1 John 3:14). Doing so demonstrates that God brought us to life and that we know him (1 John 4:7).

For Reflection and Discussion

Use these two pages to respond to the following questions, to record your prayers to God, and/or to prepare to process this information with others.

1. What makes God worthy of your love and your obedience?
2. Are there ways you express hostility toward God (James 4:4)? How can you fight against those tendencies?
3. How can you express your love for God in concrete ways? For others?

Guide for Meeting with Others

Open with Prayer

Recite Memory Verses

For Discussion

1. Listening and Prayer

   a. Read Romans 1:18–20, 2 Timothy 3:16–17, and Hebrews 1:1–2. Identify and explain the ways that God speaks to us. To what extent do you faithfully listen to and obey God's Word? Explain.
   b. Describe your prayer life in detail, both individually and as you pray with others. What steps can you take to grow in your prayer life?

2. Faith, Hope, and Love

   a. Read 1 John 1:9 and 2 Timothy 2:13. Why is God worthy of your trust? Which of God's promises are most meaningful to you at this point in your life?
   b. Read Psalm 33:16–17 and 1 Peter 1:21. What is hope? In what ways do you inappropriately hope in other people and things? In what ways do you want to hope in God to a greater extent?
   c. Read Matthew 22:34–40 and John 14:21; 15:9–10. What does it mean to love God? What are some of the ways you want to express your love for God and Jesus Christ?

3. Responding to God

   a. What part of the lessons on the preceding pages did you find to be the most helpful or challenging? Why?
   b. Name one or more of your desires that you want to bring to God in prayer (for yourself and/or for others).

Pray for One Another

Notes

Notes

Unit Seven:
We Center Our Lives on God (Part II)

Overview

Introduction

At the beginning of the last unit, I stated that the ultimate, unifying goal of the Christian life is to be God-centered in all that we do. There, I outlined five ways we do that. In this unit, I outline five additional ways. Because he is the one true God and in accordance with Scripture, we are to:

- imitate God in conformity to the likeness of Jesus.
- worship God as the one who is more valuable and worthy than anyone or anything else.
- glorify God as the one who is supremely good and important.
- enjoy God as the one who eternally satisfies our deepest desires.
- obey God in humble submission to his supreme authority.

This unit explores the question, "What other ways do we experience and express God-centeredness in our lives?"

Reading

Read lessons thirty-one through thirty-five.

Memory Verses

- "But as the one who called you is holy, you also are to be holy in all your conduct; for it is written, 'Be holy, because I am holy.'" (1 Pet. 1:15–16)
- "You reveal the path of life to me; in your presence is abundant joy; at your right hand are eternal pleasures." (Ps. 16:11)

31. Imitate God

The desire to imitate other people is one of our strongest instincts, and it begins soon after we are born. Newborn babies imitate the facial expressions of their moms and dads, particularly their looks of joy. Next, they learn to imitate the sounds they hear and the behaviors they see. In time, they are singing and dancing like their favorite pop stars or running and jumping like their favorite sports heroes. Each of us seeks to imitate others.

We quickly realize that imitation has a moral dimension. We value what others value, say what others say, and do what others do. As we imitate, we face the moral implications of each act. At times, we choose to imitate others who are self-centered, greedy, and seductive. At other times, we choose to imitate those who are self-sacrificial, wise, and devoted to God's Word.

The problem is that no human besides Jesus can serve as our ultimate reference point, because Romans 3:23 is clear: "For all have sinned and fall short of the glory of God." Given that we cannot help but imitate, to whom should we ultimately look to determine our character?

1. We imitate God the Father.

- "Therefore, be imitators of God, as dearly loved children." (Eph. 5:1)
- "For it is written, 'Be holy, because I am holy.'" (1 Pet. 1:16)
- "Dear friends, let us love one another, because love is from God, and everyone who loves has been born of God and knows God. The one who does not love does not know God, because God is love." (1 John 4:7–8)

As children of God the Father, we seek to become like him (Eph. 5:1). There are certain aspects of God's being that are unique to him alone; for example, he is all-knowing (1 John 3:20) and eternal (Ps. 90:2). But as we study the Bible, we search for aspects of God's character that he wants us to emulate. For example, in 1 Peter 1:13–16, we seek to be holy because God is holy. In 1 John 4:7–8, we learn that God is love, love is from

God, and we, therefore, must love one another. Doing so demonstrates that we are indeed his children (1 John 3:10, 14).

2. We imitate Jesus Christ.

- "For those he foreknew he also predestined to be conformed to the image of his Son." (Rom. 8:29)
- "Walk in love, as Christ also loved us and gave himself for us, a sacrificial and fragrant offering to God." (Eph. 5:2)

Just as we imitate God the Father, we also imitate Jesus Christ. God set his affection on us from eternity past so that we would "be conformed to the image of his Son" (Rom. 8:29). We walk in love as Jesus loved us—seen most clearly in Jesus's sacrificial death on our behalf (Eph. 5:2). "Walking in love" is one example of imitating Jesus, and love is our core motivation as we do the good works God has prepared for us (Eph. 2:10).

3. We imitate by the Holy Spirit.

> But the fruit of the Spirit is love, joy, peace, patience, kindness, goodness, faithfulness, gentleness, and self-control. The law is not against such things. (Gal. 5:22–23)

The Spirit guides and empowers Christians, but we must "keep in step" with him (Gal. 5:25), which involves turning away from the works of our sinful disposition (Gal. 5:19–21) and pursuing godly character (Gal. 5:22–23). As we cooperate with the Holy Spirit, he produces in us the transformation that God requires.

Life with God

We cannot imitate what we do not see and hear on a regular basis. Therefore, we identify Christians we want to imitate and move closer to them (Heb. 13:7). More foundationally, we recommit ourselves to being men and women who study, cherish, and obey the Word of God. In it we see "the light of the knowledge of God's glory in the face of Jesus Christ" (2 Cor. 4:6), and we imitate accordingly.

For Reflection and Discussion

Use these two pages to respond to the following questions, to record your prayers to God, and/or to prepare to process this information with others.

1. In what ways are you tempted to imitate the wrong people and their wrong value systems? What makes doing so attractive?
2. What aspects of Jesus's character do you want to imitate? How would that translate into changed behavior?
3. Name at least one Christian role model in your life. In what ways do you want to imitate him or her? How would that translate into observable behavior?

32. Worship God

God instructs us in a variety of ways: to use our spiritual gifts (1 Pet. 4:10–11), to give financially (2 Cor. 9:7), and to love one another (1 John 4:7). These are concrete acts of obedience, and each is critically important. But what is the most important *motivation* for Christians? Along with loving God and his Son, Jesus Christ (Matt. 22:37–38; John 14:15), the answer is worship.

But given our sinful disposition, and given our sinful character and actions, we value people and things more than God our Creator. To do so is the essence of sin; to do so is idolatry:

- "For all the gods of the peoples are idols, but the LORD made the heavens." (Ps. 96:5)
- "They exchanged the truth of God for a lie, and worshiped and served what has been created instead of the Creator, who is praised forever. Amen." (Rom. 1:25)

When we value someone or something more than God, we express it in concrete actions, whether we serve the gods of money, sex, vanity, power, or possessions.

What, then, does it mean to worship God? Worship is an internal experience (something that happens in our hearts) and an external expression (something that happens in our words and actions) of enjoying God's supreme value or worth.[53] How do we experience and express our worship?

1. We worship God the Father.

- "Our Lord and God, you are worthy to receive glory and honor and power, because you have created all things, and by your will they exist and were created." (Rev. 4:11)
- "But an hour is coming, and is now here, when the true worshipers will worship the Father in Spirit and in truth. Yes, the Father wants such people to worship him." (John 4:23)

---

[53] John Piper's *Desiring God* demonstrates that the essence of worship is enjoying God above all—being satisfied in him. See Psalm 16:11.

Just as Jesus directs us to love God the Father (Matt. 22:37–38), so he directs us to worship him (Matt. 4:10; John 4:23–24). Christians agree with the heavenly worshipers that God is worthy to receive glory, honor, and power, precisely because he is the Creator (Acts 14:15; Rev. 4:11).

2. We worship Jesus Christ.

- "Worthy is the Lamb who was slaughtered to receive power and riches and wisdom and strength and honor and glory and blessing!" (Rev. 5:12)
- "And they sang a new song: 'You are worthy to take the scroll and to open its seals, because you were slaughtered, and you purchased people for God by your blood from every tribe and language and people and nation.'" (Rev. 5:9)

Like God the Father, Jesus is worthy for humans and angels alike to experience and express his ultimate worth (Matt. 28:9; Heb. 1:6; Rev. 5:12). One of the many reasons we worship him is that he died for us—purchasing us for God, freeing us from our sins, and enabling us to persevere to the end (Rev. 1:5; 5:9; 12:11).

3. We worship by the Holy Spirit.

> For we are the circumcision, the ones who worship by the Spirit of God, boast in Christ Jesus, and do not put confidence in the flesh. (Phil. 3:3)

One of the ministries of the Holy Spirit is that he facilitates and empowers our worship (Phil. 3:3). When people worship God, the Spirit is there (Acts 13:2; Rev. 4:5). We honor the Spirit's work in our lives by doing the things he prompts us to do.

Life with God

We worship God the Father and Jesus Christ by the power of the Holy Spirit (Phil. 3:3; Rev. 5:13–14; 7:10). Worship occurs in spirit and truth (John 4:23–24), expresses itself in song (Ps. 66:4), and is mingled with thanksgiving (Rev. 11:16–17). Ultimately, we present our bodies to God as a living sacrifice, because he is worth it (Rom. 12:1).

For Reflection and Discussion

Use these two pages to respond to the following questions, to record your prayers to God, and/or to prepare to process this information with others.

1. What makes God so valuable and worthy of praise?
2. In what ways are you tempted to value other people and things more than God? How does this express itself in your words and actions?
3. How do you want worship to express itself in your life? "Because I value God above all, I will _____."

33. Glorify God

"What is important to you?" You might answer in any number of ways: family members, friends, or a church.

But if I asked, "What is *supremely* important to you?" there is only one appropriate answer. Christians confess that God—and God alone—is supremely important (Ps. 86:8–10; Isa. 48:9–11; Luke 2:14). This is the starting point to understanding the concept of God's glory.

God's glory is his supreme importance and excellence, an intrinsic quality that he allows people to see.[54] With that as a starting point, some of the ways Scripture traces out this concept become clear:

- God possesses glory as an intrinsic quality of his supreme importance and excellence (Eph. 1:17).
- God displays his glory through his image-bearers, creation, and saving works (Pss. 8:5; 19:1; 79:9).
- We ascribe glory to God by seeing, savoring, and expressing God's glory (1 Cor. 10:31).
- God receives glory in that he is honored and celebrated as the one who is supremely glorious (Matt. 5:16; Rev. 4:11).

How, in particular, do we experience and express God's glory?

1. We glorify God the Father.

- "He predestined us to be adopted as sons through Jesus Christ for himself, according to the good pleasure of his will, to the praise of his glorious grace that he lavished on us in the Beloved One." (Eph. 1:5–6)
- "In him we have also received an inheritance, because we were predestined according to the plan of the one who works out everything in agreement with the purpose of his will, so that we who had already put our hope in Christ might bring praise to his glory." (Eph. 1:11–12)

---

[54] Morgan's excellent chapter, "Toward a Theology of the Glory of God," was pivotal in helping shape this lesson.

God the Father is glorious in his nature and in all his actions. In Ephesians 1, for example, we respond to God's saving work in our lives (such as choosing us and adopting us) by praising "his glorious grace" (v. 6) and "bring[ing] praise to his glory" (v. 12). Indeed, all his work draws us to such a response (Acts 11:18; Rom. 15:5–6; Eph. 3:21), particularly in and through Jesus.

2. We glorify Jesus Christ.

- "Jesus replied to them, 'The hour has come for the Son of Man to be glorified.'" (John 12:23)
- "So that the name of our Lord Jesus will be glorified by you, and you by him, according to the grace of our God and the Lord Jesus Christ." (2 Thess. 1:12)

Jesus is glorious, revealing the glory of God the Father (John 1:14, 18; Heb. 1:3). We see Jesus's glory in the incarnation (John 1:14), his death (John 12:23–28), his resurrection (1 Pet. 1:21), his ascension (1 Tim. 3:16), and his return (Matt. 25:31). What could be more important and worthy of our attention (2 Thess. 1:9–12)?

3. We glorify by the Holy Spirit.

> We all, with unveiled faces, are looking as in a mirror at the glory of the Lord and are being transformed into the same image from glory to glory; this is from the Lord who is the Spirit. (2 Cor. 3:18)

The Holy Spirit is glorious (1 Pet. 4:14). His work helps us to see the glory of God, and we glorify the Father and the Son accordingly (John 16:14; Acts 7:55; 2 Cor. 3:18; Eph. 1:13–14).

Life with God

We glorify God by expressing his supreme importance and excellence as we cry out to him for help (Ps. 50:15), thank him (Ps. 86:12), celebrate God's Word (Acts 13:48), use our spiritual gifts (1 Pet. 4:10–11), and suffer righteously (1 Pet. 4:16). Any time we see and express God's supreme importance, he is glorified (1 Cor. 10:31). And one day, we will be with him in glory (in heaven), in glorified bodies forever (Ps. 73:24; Rom. 8:17).

For Reflection and Discussion

Use these two pages to respond to the following questions, to record your prayers to God, and/or to prepare to process this information with others.

1. What makes God so excellent in his being, thoughts, words, and actions?
2. In what ways are you tempted to glorify other people and things? What would it look like for you to turn away from these thoughts and actions and turn back to God?
3. How can you live out the truth that God is the most important part of your life?

34. Enjoy God

All human beings seek pleasure. This search for pleasure drives our decision making. From relatively minor decisions (like choosing the toppings on a pizza) to significant decisions (like choosing a spouse), we seek to maximize our pleasure.

The way we seek pleasure matters to God.[55] While there may be no moral significance in choosing an apple instead of a banana for a snack, there is a profound difference whether we enjoy sex outside the context of marriage or within it. In this case, the question is not simply what we enjoy but also in what context (inside or outside marriage) and for what reasons.

Thus, the most important question is "Who or what do we enjoy above all?" Or, put differently, "Who or what do we ultimately seek to satisfy our deepest longings?"

The way we answer those questions identifies our ultimate object of joy, which is simultaneously our object of worship. Christians seek joy in that which is ultimately pleasurable. How so?

1. We rejoice in God the Father.

- "You reveal the path of life to me; in your presence is abundant joy; at your right hand are eternal pleasures." (Ps. 16:11)
- "And not only that, but we also rejoice in God through our Lord Jesus Christ, through whom we have now received this reconciliation." (Rom. 5:11)

Whether it is food or family or friends, God gives good gifts that he wants us to enjoy (Acts 14:17; James 1:17). But God alone provides fullness of joy (as opposed to superficial, trivial pleasures), and God alone provides eternal joy (as opposed to pleasures that come to an end) (Ps. 16:11).[56] Knowing God

---

[55] See Piper's *The Dangerous Duty of Delight* for an introduction to seeking joy in God and his *Desiring God* for an extended treatment.
[56] A frequent observation in Piper's preaching and teaching ministry.

through Jesus Christ is the greatest joy of all (Rom. 5:11)—a joy we will experience fully and eternally in heaven (Rev. 19:6–7).

2. We rejoice in Jesus Christ.

- "I have told you these things so that my joy may be in you and your joy may be complete." (John 15:11)
- "Though you have not seen him, you love him; though not seeing him now, you believe in him, and you rejoice with inexpressible and glorious joy, because you are receiving the goal of your faith, the salvation of your souls." (1 Pet. 1:8–9)

Jesus rejoiced in his relationship with God, and Jesus came so our joy would be full (Luke 10:21; John 15:11). How do we experience and express our joy? We rejoice in Jesus (Phil. 4:4), we obey Jesus (John 15:10–11), and we anticipate Jesus's return, resulting in the salvation of our souls (1 Pet. 1:3–9).

3. We rejoice by the Holy Spirit.

- "But the fruit of the Spirit is love, joy…" (Gal. 5:22)
- "And the disciples were filled with joy and the Holy Spirit." (Acts 13:52)

From the time we first receive God's Word (1 Thess. 1:6), the Holy Spirit produces joy in the lives of Christians (Gal. 5:22). As we rejoice in God and in Jesus, the Spirit leads us to rejoice in ministry that is faithful to God's Word, even in the face of great opposition and suffering (Acts 5:40–41; 13:52; 16:22–25; Rom. 5:3–5).

Life with God

Joy is not simply an emotion. It is also a choice to see and to savor that which is worth celebrating. We rejoice in God himself (Ps. 16:11), in Jesus (Phil. 4:4), in God's Word (Ps. 1:1–2), and when we hear that other Christians are obeying the truth (2 John 4). No one can take these joys from us, but we must fix our eyes on God and the future he guarantees to realize that joy (Rom. 5:2; Rev. 19:7).

For Reflection and Discussion

Use these two pages to respond to the following questions, to record your prayers to God, and/or to prepare to process this information with others.

1. How are you tempted to seek pleasure in inappropriate, God-dishonoring ways?
2. How do Christians seek joy in practical ways?
3. What interferes with your joy in God? How can you remove these obstacles and experience more joy in your relationship with God?

35. Obey God

We experience and express God-centeredness in a variety of ways.

- Faith says to God, "I will trust you because you alone are ultimately trustworthy."
- Hope says to God, "I will hope in you because you alone shape and guarantee the future."
- Love says to God, "I will love you because you are the most desirable and worthy being in the universe."

And because we recognize God's ultimate authority in our lives, we obey him—in thought, word, and deed. How does obedience express itself in our lives?

1. We obey God the Father.

> Everyone who believes that Jesus is the Christ has been born of God, and everyone who loves the Father also loves the one born of him. This is how we know that we love God's children: when we love God and obey his commands. For this is what love for God is: to keep his commands. And his commands are not a burden. (1 John 5:1–3)

Before we became Christians, each of us was dead in our sins (Eph. 2:1), unresponsive to God, to his Word, and therefore to his will. But God brought us to life (Eph. 2:4–7). We demonstrate that we are alive to God as we express our belief that Jesus is the Christ (the Anointed One of God) and as we love God (1 John 5:1). Loving God, obeying him, and loving the children of God are at the center of the Christian faith. These commands are inseparable (vv. 2–3). God's commands are not burdensome (v. 3), precisely because Christians delight in doing God's will.

2. We obey Jesus Christ.

> "As the Father has loved me, I have also loved you. Remain in my love. If you keep my commands you will remain in my love, just as I have kept my Father's commands and remain in his love. I have told you these things so that my joy may be in you and your joy may be complete." (John 15:9–11)

As the Father has loved Jesus, so Jesus loves his people (v. 9). Jesus commands us to abide or remain within the confines of his love and guidance (v. 9; Jude 21). Obeying Jesus is the way we abide or remain within his love (v. 10). In this life, we will never obey him perfectly, but Jesus's obedience to his Father is our standard and example (v. 10). Jesus spoke these words to impart his joy in us and to fulfill our joy (v. 11).

3. We obey by the Holy Spirit.

- "If you love me, you will keep my commands. And I will ask the Father, and he will give you another Counselor to be with you forever. He is the Spirit of truth. The world is unable to receive him because it doesn't see him or know him. But you do know him, because he remains with you and will be in you." (John 14:15–17)
- "I will place my Spirit within you and cause you to follow my statutes and carefully observe my ordinances." (Ezek. 36:27)

We express our love for Jesus by obeying him (v. 15), but we cannot do so without help. Jesus promised that God would send a Counselor or Helper, who is the Holy Spirit (v. 16). God did this for the entire church (Acts 2:1–4). He is described as the Spirit of truth, the one who dwells with and within Christians, and the one who helps us to know and obey God's truth (Ezek. 36:27; John 14:17; 15:26; 2 Thess. 2:13).

Life with God

If we love God and his Son Jesus Christ, we will obey their commands in Scripture (John 14:15; 1 John 5:3) by the power of the Holy Spirit (Col. 1:8). And so we pray like the psalmist: "Help me stay on the path of your commands, for I take pleasure in it" (Ps. 119:35). That prayer reflects the ultimate desire of all believers. Yet when we disobey, we turn from our sin and turn back to Jesus, the Good Shepherd who lays his life down for his sheep (John 10:14–15).

For Reflection and Discussion

Use these two pages to respond to the following questions, to record your prayers to God, and/or to prepare to process this information with others.

1. In what areas of your life do you struggle to obey God?
2. In those areas, what makes it so difficult, at times, to obey? In other words, what makes disobedience so tempting?
3. What are strategies for learning to become more obedient? What advice would you have for a fellow Christian?

Guide for Meeting with Others

Open with Prayer

Recite Memory Verses

For Discussion

1. Imitate, Worship, and Glorify God

    a. Read Ephesians 5:1–2 and Romans 8:29. What are some of the characteristics of God and Jesus Christ we *should* try to imitate? What are some of their characteristics that we should *not* try to imitate (to avoid pretending to be God)?
    b. Read Romans 12:1–2 and Revelation 5:11–14. What is worship? What makes God so valuable and worthy of praise?
    c. Read Matthew 5:16 and Ephesians 1:6, 12, 14. What is God's glory? What does it mean to glorify God? In what ways are you tempted to glorify people and things other than God himself?

2. Enjoy and Obey God

    a. Read Psalm 16:11 and John 15:11. What is joy? What does it mean to have joy *in God*, and why is that so important in your life? What about God makes you rejoice?
    b. Read 1 John 5:1–3 and John 15:9–11. How do you know when God is asking you to do something or not to do something? What are various strategies for learning to become more obedient?

3. Responding to God

    a. What part of the lessons on the preceding pages did you find to be the most helpful or challenging? Why?
    b. Name one or more of your desires that you want to bring to God in prayer (for yourself and/or for others).

Pray for One Another

Notes

Notes

References

Carson, D. A. *Matthew*. In Longman III and Garland (eds.) *Matthew and Mark* (rev. ed.). Grand Rapids, MI: Zondervan, 2010.

Carson, D. A. *The Difficult Doctrine of the Love of God*. Wheaton, IL: Crossway Books, 2000.

Carson, D. A. "What Is the Gospel?—Revisited." In Storms and Taylor (eds.). *For the Fame of God's Name: Essays in Honor of John Piper*. Wheaton, IL: Crossway, 2010.

Chandler, Matt and Wilson, Jared. *The Explicit Gospel*. Wheaton, IL: Crossway, 2012.

Crossway. *ESV Study Bible (ESVSB)*. Wheaton, IL: Crossway, 2008.

Dever, Mark. *What Is a Healthy Church?* Wheaton, IL: Crossway Books, 2007.

DeYoung, Kevin & Gilbert, Greg. *What Is the Mission of the Church?: Making Sense of Social Justice, Shalom, and the Great Commission*. Wheaton, IL: Crossway, 2011.

Edwards, James. *The Gospel according to Mark*. Grand Rapids, MI; Eerdmans, 2002.

Gilbert, Greg. *What Is the Gospel?* Wheaton, IL: Crossway, 2010.

Grudem, Wayne and Grudem, Elliot (ed.). *Christian Beliefs: Twenty Basics Every Christian Should Know*. Grand Rapids, MI: Zondervan, 2005.

Harris, Murray. *The Second Epistle to the Corinthians: A Commentary on the Greek Text*. Grand Rapids, MI: Eerdmans, 2005.

Holman Bible Publishers. *CSB Study Bible (CSBSB)*. Nashville, TN: Holman Bible Publishers, 2017.

Köstenberger, Andreas. *Commentary on 1–2 Timothy and Titus*. Nashville, TN: Holman Reference, 2017.

Millar, J. Gary. *Calling on the Name of the Lord: A Biblical Theology of Prayer*. Downers Grove, IL: InterVarsity, 2016.

Moo, Douglas. *Galatians*. Grand Rapids, MI: Baker Academic, 2013.

Moo, Douglas. *The Letter to the Romans* (2nd ed.). Grand Rapids, MI: Eerdmans, 2018.

Moo, Douglas and Moo, Jonathan. *Creation Care: A Biblical Theology of the Natural World*. Grand Rapids, MI: Zondervan, 2018.

Morgan, Christopher. "How Does the Trinity's Love Shape Our Love for One Another." In Morgan (ed.) *The Love of God*. Wheaton, IL: Crossway, 2016.

Morgan, Christopher. "Toward a Theology of the Glory of God." In Morgan and Peterson (eds.) *The Glory of God*. Wheaton, IL: Crossway, 2010.

Osborne, Grant. *Matthew*. Grand Rapids, MI: Zondervan, 2010.

Peterson, David. *Possessed by God: A New Testament Theology of Sanctification and Holiness*. Downers Grove, IL: InterVarsity, 2001.

Piper, John. *Battling Unbelief: Defeating Sin with Superior Pleasure*. Colorado Springs, CO: Multnomah, 2007.

Piper, John. *Desiring God: Meditations of a Christian Hedonist*. Colorado Springs, CO: Multnomah, 2011.

Piper, John. *The Dangerous Duty of Delight: Daring to Make God Your Greatest Desire*. Colorado Springs, CO: Multnomah, 2001.

Schreiner, Thomas. *Galatians*. Grand Rapids, MI: Zondervan, 2010.

Schreiner, Thomas. *New Testament Theology: Magnifying God in Christ*. Grand Rapids, MI: Baker, 2008.

Zondervan. *NIV Biblical Theology Study Bible (NIVBTSB)*. Grand Rapids, MI: Zondervan, 2018.

Acknowledgments

I completed this book at roughly the same time I completed my first book, *Start*. Therefore, the list of people I thanked there are largely the same group who encouraged me on this project. Of all those people, I am particularly grateful for:

- Drs. Gene Smillie, Craig Long, and Neal Huddleston, for their detailed feedback on this manuscript.
- Jeff Van Etten, for his helpful suggestions throughout.
- Christi McGuire, for her steady and stabilizing presence as my editor.
- Hannah Vogltanz, for her great skill as my proofreader.
- Renée Yearwood, for her excellent internal and external design work.
- Lyndsey Simala, for striving with me to live out the vision of this book, both in our home and in our church.

"I always thank my God for you because of the grace of God given to you in Christ Jesus, that you were enriched in him in every way, in all speech and all knowledge."
1 Corinthians 1:4–5

www.ingramcontent.com/pod-product-compliance
Lightning Source LLC
Chambersburg PA
CBHW071157070526
44584CB00019B/2829